SUCCESSFUL

SEA ANGLING

SUCCESSFUL

SEA ANGLING

Trevor Housby

BLANDFORD

To my son, Russell Housby

Blandford
An imprint of Cassell
Villiers House, 41/47 Strand, London WC2N 5JE

First published 1990

Distributed in the United States by
Sterling Publishing Co. Inc.
387 Park Avenue South, New York , NY 10016–8810

Distributed in Australia by
Capricorn Link (Australia) Pty Ltd
PO Box 665, Lane Cove, NSW 2066

British Library Cataloguing in Publication Data
Housby, Trevor 1939–
Successful sea angling.
1. Sea angling
I. Title
799.16

ISBN 0–7137–2117 0

Typeset by Fakenham Photosetting Ltd
Fakenham, Norfolk
Printed and bound in Great Britain by
Courie · International, Tiptree, Essex

Contents

Introduction

Anglers today have the advantage of a full range of weekly and monthly magazines and a growing number of video films to learn from. Through these most anglers can gain a working knowledge of tackle, terminal rigs, knots and methods. But what many lack is the confidence, experience and know-how to get the best out of a fishing expedition. The best way to learn after actual experience is through enjoyable reading.

Cold hard facts, although important, just do not get the whole message across. What is needed is a book covering not only the basic facts but the thought processes behind successful angling trips; a book that sets the scene, tells the story, and gives the reasons for changing terminal tackle. In this way anglers will learn to assess each day's fishing and adjust the tackle accordingly.

Take cod as just one example. Probably the most popular and most widespread of British fish, cod can be caught successfully and enjoyably in a wide variety of ways: feathering, bottom fishing, pirk fishing, wire-line fishing, with or without attractor spoons. Any angler faced with so many options is hard pressed to know just what technique to use in a particular situation. This book will, I hope, sort out these problems by referring to actual days of fishing to illustrate the tackle required.

Sea angling is a growing sport. A similar explosion occurred in coarse fishing during the 1950s and 1960s, when many anglers discovered for the first time that they could set out to catch a particular fish. This is, I believe, the first book on sea angling to explain just how and why specimen-hunting approaches work in salt water.

Trevor Housby

1

Bass

Bass are among the most sought after of sea fish, their reputation as a sporting and table fish being second to none. They have, however, suffered greatly at the hands of commercial fishing. Because they command an extremely high price in the European fish markets, their stocks have been depleted beyond all reason. For example in Ireland, once a Mecca for visiting bass anglers, the government was forced to put a stop to all inshore commercial fishing. Even now, some years after the ban, the fish have not returned in any quantity. But there are signs that stocks are beginning to improve, and it is to be hoped that this trend will continue.

Bass are slow to grow and even slower to reach maturity. It may take an individual fish eight or more years to reach a weight of 3 lb (1.4 kg). Really large bass are usually close to 20 years old, and such fish may have spawned only a few times during their mature years. Seen in the water, a big bass looks every inch a bold fighter.

The species is commonest south of a line drawn between the Wash and the west coast of Wales. A few fish penetrate northwards as far as the Scottish coast, and there is a theory that these come round the north of Ireland on an arm of the Gulf Stream. Records show that the occasional monster bass is captured off the Antrim coast of Northern Ireland, which may be evidence of the route taken by the Scottish specimens. Both Essex and Suffolk have produced huge bass, and the original record was held for many years by a bass taken off Felixstowe. An obliging species, bass can be caught in a variety of methods and baits.

SPINNING

On rocky coastlines or steep-to-shingle banks, bass often fall to artificial lures. For this kind of fishing a 10 or 11 ft (3 or 3.3 m) carp-style rod and medium-sized fixed-spool reel should be used. At present, the most suitable reel is the wide-drummed Shimano BioMaster, which has a spool designed specifically for

BASS

An unmistakable fish, the bass belongs to the perch family and, like its freshwater cousin, has a large, spiny dorsal fin. Its extremely compact body is covered with hard, firmly attached scales, which give the fish a rugged yet streamlined appearance. Bass, particularly small bass, vary in colour from bluish-grey to greenish-grey, with brilliantly burnished silver flanks and white underparts. Some very large bass have dusky grey backs and tarnished silver sides. In prime condition a bass is muscular and heavy in the shoulder.

Most rod-caught bass range from 2 to 6 lb (0.9–2.7 kg). A fish weighing over 12 lb (5.4 kg) is an outstanding specimen. There is evidence, however, that under favourable conditions bass can reach weights well over 20 lb (9.1 kg).

Bass are mainly a rough-water species which thrives in heavy seas and in areas subject to tide rips or overfalls. Rocks and reefs which cause the sea to churn and foam are ideal places to hunt for bass, and the rougher the water the better the chance of catching good-sized fish. A small sandy beach flanked by rock often makes a great shore-fishing venue. In Ireland and Wales, long, open storm-beaches are favourite places for the shore angler to try for bass.

Although bass can be caught at any time of year, the bass-fishing season effectively lasts from mid April until early October. During very mild winters, bass in West Country waters may stay throughout the winter as well, but as a rule the first cold weather drives them into deep water away from the coast. In my experience the best months for bass are May–June and September–October.

distance casting. Loaded with 10 or 12 lb (4.5 or 5.4 kg) line, it is capable of casting a lure further than reels with a spool of more conventional size.

The choice of lures is up to the individual angler. Most use long wobbling spoons of the Abu Toby type. The Abu Koster spoon is another good fish catcher. Both spinners are obtainable in a heavy metal version for ultra-long-distance casting. This type of lure is best used over deep, snag-free areas. However, for catching bass in deep rock gullies or over sunken rock ledges, a plug bait is the most useful. Plugs can be obtained as floaters, slow sinkers and deep divers. For fishing heavily snagged areas, the floating or slow-sinking patterns are best. The floating pattern is particularly useful. When retrieved, it dives and wiggles, but stop the retrieve and it will float to the surface. This means that it can be cast out beyond a snag on a weed patch, worked back and then floated over the obstruction.

FIGURE 1   A jointed plug bait. With light tackle the weight of the plug bait will be sufficient for casting.

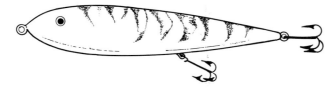

FIGURE 2   A Rapala plug bait. For bass a magnum pattern is the best bet.

Plugs, like spinners, come in a multitude of sizes, patterns and colours. In my experience the jointed blue and silver plug is the most effective (see Fig. 1). Other anglers, though, prefer single-section plugs such as the Shakespeare Big S, or the long, slim Rapala (see Fig. 2). An artificial lure is only as good as the angler using it. There is a lot more to spinning than casting and retrieving, and the ability to make a lure work well is nine tenths of the battle.

To attract and catch bass, the moving lure must simulate a natural or badly damaged live fish. Like most predators, bass hunt by eyesight and smell and by detecting vibrations. A lure which sends out a good vibration will normally catch better than one which does not vary in speed or direction. The answer is to vary the rate of retrieve and at the same time vary the angle of the rod tip. This will cause the lure to bob and weave through the water (see Fig. 3), with luck sending out signals to any bass in the area.

Good, well-balanced spinners and plugs are never cheap. There are hundreds of cheap lures, most designed to catch anglers rather than fish. Lure collecting can become an obsession, and this tendency should be avoided. If you carry a box crammed with lures, you will spend all day changing them. It is better to stick to two or three tried-and-tested patterns, for in this way you will learn how to get the best out of each lure.

For fishing normal tide runs, the weight of the spinner is usually sufficient. In big tides, however, additional lead may be necessary to hold the lure down. The best lead for this purpose is the Wye lead (see Fig. 4). Normally employed by salmon anglers, this useful weight is perfectly adaptable for use in salt water.

Many anglers still use a wire trace for all bass spinning. This is unnecessary, for bass do not have teeth and a plain nylon trace is quite adequate. Also, the flexibility of the nylon allows the bait to work more freely, which is an important factor when the bass are finicky.

When they do decide to take an artificial lure, bass normally hit it with a bang. To make certain of hooking a taking fish, the hooks on a plug or spoon must be kept sharp and rust free. At the end of each day, lures should be washed off in fresh tap water and then lightly oiled to stop rust setting in. Equally important is to dry out the compartments of the lure box, and a sachet of silica gel should be kept in the box to absorb moisture. It is obtainable from camera shops.

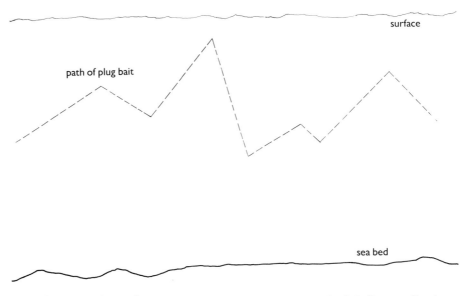

FIGURE 3　A varied rate of retrieve imparts maximum action to a plug bait. Bass usually take their bait in a savage fashion.

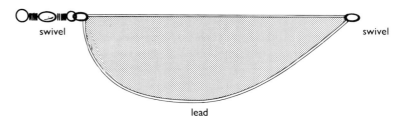

FIGURE 4　A Wye lead, with swivel at both ends.

Although mostly used by shore anglers, spinning techniques can also be used by dinghy anglers. Dinghy fishing is particularly effective for catching bass over offshore sand or shingle banks.

TROLLING

When big bass congregate round banks that are subject to really heavy tides, trolling is often the only way to catch them. For this style of angling a Mevagissey Red Gill is still the best bait. These lifelike rubber sand eels come in a wide variety of colours, but for bass blue-and-silver, green-and-silver and white seem to be the most effective. I discovered the killing properties of a white imitation eel by accident. I had been in Mevagissey and called in at the Red Gill factory. The late Alex Ingram, inventor of the Red Gill, was an old friend, and handed me a batch of uncoloured Red Gills. Later that week, I was on my way to the shingle bank off the Needles lighthouse. This was a great place for bass and we had rigged up a typical trolling trace. Instead of using a conventional coloured eel, I decided to try an uncoloured (i.e. white) version.

Minutes after starting to troll, I hit a 9 lb (4.1 kg) bass. One fish doesn't prove anything, so I tried again. The next fish was smaller but, at around 5 lb (2.3 kg), perfectly acceptable. For the third time I ran the bait back into the churning white water and as the line tightened, the rod was practically ripped out of my hands. With my third fish in the boat, my companion still hadn't had a touch. The white eel used in the yellow water was clearly just what the fish wanted. Naturally, I handed my companion one of my new Red Gills and soon we were both catching fish. Since then I have caught hundreds of fine bass on white eels. They seem to be particularly deadly in dirty water where visibility is down to a minimum.

As an alternative to the rubber eel, a large Rapala plug lure can be extremely effective. These are costly, but worth every penny. Again, blue-and-silver or mackerel coloured Rapalas seem to make the best fish catchers. They are selective fish catchers unlike the Red Gill, which catches bass of all sizes, Rapala lures seem to attract only the better-quality fish.

Most anglers don't buy a rod specifically for trolling. Instead they make do with a 20 or 30 lb (9.1–13.6 kg) class boat rod and a 4–0 multiplying reel. This may sound heavy for trolling, but bear in mind that you may have to use leads of 6–12 oz (170–340 g), depending on tide strength. A wire line will cut down on weight, but if wire is used your rod must have a roller tip ring. The finest line for general trolling is Dacron or Sea Ranger. Nylon has too much inbuilt stretch and when used for trolling it may contract sufficiently to crack or strain the reel spool. With non-stretch Dacron this doesn't occur. Equally important is the fact that this sort of line keeps you in direct contact with the lure. With Dacron, when a fish snaps up the bait it usually hooks itself solidly. With nylon, however, the elasticity of the line causes some of the fish to bounce off and escape.

DRIFT FISHING

Where the tide runs over a sunken reef, drift fishing can be a deadly method for catching bass. Many anglers simply use a set of bright tinsel or mackerel feathers to catch their fish. Feathering is good when the fish are present in large shoals. On days when the fish are more widespread, the only bait that will work consistently is a live sand eel fished on leadless tackle. The point of the hook (a fairly long-shanked Aberdeen-style pattern is best) is passed through the gills of the live eel and gently nicked into the skin of the bait's belly. Alternatively, the bait can be hooked through the back just behind the head (see Fig. 5). In both cases the hooking method leaves the eel lively enough to swim naturally.

For this style of fishing, a spinning rod and fixed-spool reel should be used. With the bale arm of the reel in the open position, the movement of the swimming eel will take out line. Bass hit a naturally swimming eel with ferocity and most are hooked well inside the mouth.

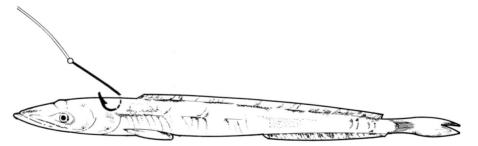

FIGURE 5   Back-hooked sand eel. Livebaiting is often very successful, for bass are active hunters.

DINGHY FISHING WITH A ROLLING LEGER

When bass move in to feed over comparatively shallow inshore grounds, dinghy fishing with live tackle can be great fun. Over the years I have tried a variety of techniques for inshore bass. The most consistently successful method, however, has been the rolling leger. A light spinning rod and medium-sized fixed-spool reel should be used. The line breaking strain should be 8–10 lb (3.6–4.5 kg), and

the terminal tackle is made up as a simple running leger (see Fig. 6). It is essential to use a bomb-shaped lead incorporating a swivel. The lead simply slides on the reel line, being stopped by a single small-barrel swivel. Its size depends greatly on the tide flow, the aim being to weigh the bait down but not anchor it in one place. A trace of 3 ft (0.9 m) is best. I have experimented with different lengths, but find this perfect.

Normally the tackle is cast up and away from the anchored dinghy. It is then allowed to roll round until it comes to a natural halt off the stern. Once it reaches this position, it can be allowed to remain static for a minute or two. If this doesn't produce a bite, retrieve and recast. Bites can come at any time and for this reason you should hold the rod at all times.

Charter boat skipper Chris Savage holds a magnificent 11 lb 6 oz (5.2 kg) bass. Fish of this calibre normally fall to sand eel or mackerel strip.

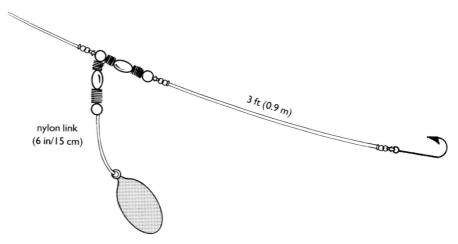

nylon link
(6 in/15 cm)

3 ft (0.9 m)

FIGURE 6 A running leger. Use an old spark plug instead of a lead when fishing over rocky ground – this is less costly!

I sometimes add a small Mepps-type spoon 6–8 in (15–20 cm) above the hook. Devoid of hooks, this simply acts as an attractor spoon, the flow of the tide being more than enough to activate the metal blade. Interestingly enough, it often produces good bites when the bait is being retrieved. I have tried a variety of hook baits on the rolling leger rig but have found ragworm or lugworm to be the best fish catchers. The hook size depends on the bait size, but I mainly use 1 or 1–0 chemically sharpened Aberdeen-style hooks.

FLOAT FISHING

Anglers fishing from piers, harbours or rock marks often take bass on float tackle. Most such fish are caught unintentionally on tackle being used for mackerel and pollack. For the shore angler willing to persevere with livebaits, float fishing can produce excellent catches of bass. The terminal tackle is a simple sliding float rig (see Fig. 7) fished on a heavy spinning or pike/carp-style rod and fixed-spool reel.

Bait is the important factor. Bass are hunters, catching most of their food live. Small fish and prawns are their favoured food. A hungry bass is not fussy about the type of fish it eats. Small wrasse, pouting, smelt, sand eels – they are all the same to the predatory bass. Smelt and wrasse are often the easiest bait fish to obtain, and of the two I prefer the silvery, cucumber-scented smelt. Dedicated anglers carry a light rod and catch their bait to order. Livebait can easily be kept in a plastic or canvas bucket to which a small aeration unit is clipped. These units are available in all good tackle shops and are essential when livebaits have to be kept in perfect condition.

Livebaits should be lip-hooked on a 1–0 or 2–0 hook and allowed to swim naturally, 2–3 ft (0.6–0.9 m) above the sea bed. Bites are normally runaway affairs but the taking bass must be allowed time to turn and begin to swallow the bait fish. The new Shimano 'baitrunner' fixed-spool reels are perfect for this style of bass fishing. They can be used with the bale arm fully closed but with the Shimano 'baitrunner' level in the operational position. A taking bass can then pull line off freely. When the fish is judged to have the bait well inside its mouth, a half turn of the reel handle will check the free-running spool, leaving the reel on fully pre-set drag, ready for striking.

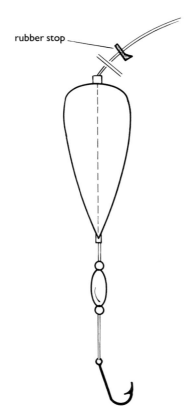

rubber stop

FIGURE 7   A sliding float. Use a rubber stop.

FREELINING DEADBAITS

This is an afterdark harbour technique which, I believe, originated at Dover. Harbour anglers often catch small, unwanted pout. These are normally brought up too fast and 'blow out' (air is forced into the swim bladder, which fills up like a balloon, making it impossible for the returned fish to dive). In this 'blown' condition the hapless pout drifts off across the surface, a perfect floating meal for the ever-watchful bass. Such baits can be used dead, and are floated on the tide on floatless, leadless tackle. Bass will seldom rise to a floating bait during the daytime, but at night they rise like trout to snatch a meal from the surface.

BEACH FISHING

A long surf beach with a good onshore wind is the perfect setting for bass fishing. The classic bass beaches are those such as Inch and Brandon in Co. Kerry, Ireland. These are long expanses of silver sand where the breakers start a long way out and the bass sweep in to feed beyond the third breaker. In the evening or at night you wade into the surf to drop your baited tackle out where the bass patrol in search of food.

For more than 20 years I have fished Co. Kerry's lovely strands. The last time, I took a huge back-up supply of salt black lugworm just in case the familiar local lugworm beds failed to produce. I need not have worried: the mudflats behind Inch beach were stiff with worm. That first evening, as I waded out into a nice creamy shallow surf, reminded me of old times. With the bait well out and the carbon beach caster pointing skyward, I remembered in particular a dark night back in the 1960s. The beach was in perfect condition. A nice heavy surf left over from a summer storm pounded in, stirring the bottom up and dislodging a multitude of edible creatures. A number of anglers were out, for lanterns twinkled along the beach and a line of expectant figures could be seen knee deep in the shallows. The wager was not on who would catch the first fish but who would catch the most.

Within ten minutes of casting I had an inquiry. There was a tentative pull which felt more like a flounder than a bass. Twice the fish tweaked at the rod tip, and I made up my mind to strike at the next tap. When it came I was ready. As the rod tip dipped I struck, expecting to feel a feeble flapping. Instead the rod hooped over as an obviously hefty bass streaked seaward. Five minutes later I walked a beautiful 9 lb (4.1 kg) bass ashore. After extracting the hooks, I admired my catch and returned it to the sea, for as a visiting angler I had no use for any bass I caught. Returning them gave me as much pleasure as retaining them and I had the satisfaction of knowing I was doing my bit for conservation.

My end tackle for beach bass presents the bait 2 ft (0.6 m) from the wired lead. In heavy surf conditions I tend to use leads incorporating longer than average lines, and consider the type used as up-tide leads to be almost perfect. The aim is to get the bait into the most productive area and hold it there. If bass are on the move they will inevitably find it. I am convinced that smell also plays an important role. In heavy surf, visibility is down to inches. In such conditions a good, juicy bait sets up its own smell, which hungry fish pick up and follow back to its source. There is already a commercially made smell additive on the market. Some claim it as a major breakthrough, but I am more conservative. I have tried it several times and have yet to find it an advantage. You can use the best additive available, but if your bait is not up to scratch in the first place, fish simply will not bite.

Beach-fishing tackle

In theory all beach rods are similar. But in practice this is far from true. Choosing an outfit depends a great deal on where you intend to do most of your fishing, as well as on the length of rod and style of reel that suit your casting style. Before purchasing tackle it pays to visit a number of tackle shops and handle a variety of rods. If you have friends who beach fish, go along with them. Watch how they cast and try out their tackle. Remember, though, that what is perfect for one person may be useless for another. Do not skimp on the price, for a beach rod has to perform a lot of rough work and cheap rods simply do not stand up to it. Most beach rods are made up in two 6 or 6½ ft (1.8 or 2 m) lengths. The rod blanks have different wall thicknesses, giving different power ratios. Usually, rods are designed to cast leads of 2–4 oz (60–115 g), 4–6 oz (115–170 g) or 6–8 oz (170–225 g). The middle type is the ideal all-round casting tool. But for bass it is best to use a light, sensitive rod of the first type.

Reels are very much a personal choice. Some anglers use multipliers, while others prefer fixed-spool sea reels. For the beginner, the latter are probably the best buy. Good reels are expensive, but they will repay the investment by giving years of excellent service. Names to look for are Shimano and Penn.

Most beach anglers today fish with comparatively light lines, 15 or 17 lb (6.8 or 7.7 kg) breaking strain being the usual choice. Remember, however, to blood-knot a 30 ft (9 m) length of 25–30 lb (11.3–13.6 kg) line to the end of the reel line. This acts as a shock leader, soaking up the power of the cast and the weight of the lead. Without this buffer, a 'break off' can easily occur, which can be extremely dangerous. Using a shock leader minimizes the chances of a serious accident as a result of a 'break-off'.

2

Cod

Most southern anglers regard cod as a winter species; a fish of those cold, drab days when the English Channel runs dark and sullen. Further north, however, cod are a summer fish. Northern cod seldom run big, but what they lack in size they more than make up for in numbers. I can recall many bumper days in Scottish waters, surrounded by magnificent scenery and with a boat full of fat northern cod. A favourite venue with many anglers is off the island of Hoy in Orkney. This is exciting fishing, for in addition to cod there are ling, coalfish and pollack. Better still, there is always the possibility of an arm-wrenching strike into a giant halibut.

Hoy cod, like most Scottish fish, are totally unsophisticated, hitting baited or unbaited pirks and spoon lures on sight. Big cod are not at all common, although fish of 15 lb (6.8 kg), occur fairly regularly. What is fascinating about Scottish and Orcadian cod fishing is the abundance of apparently suicidal fish. I recall one grey autumn day when the cloud base was so low that the top of Hoy was totally obscured. I was out with a party of Scandinavians on the *Girl Shona* out of Stromness. Despite the greyness there was little wind and skipper Michael Flett set up a drift close to the towering rock stack. Tides were comparatively slack and our heavy cod lures went straight down into 20 fathoms (55 m) of clear green water.

To say the Orcadian sea bed is rugged is an understatement. To minimize loss of tackle it is essential to 'bump' bottom, then instantly wind up 6–8 ft (1.8–2.4 m) of line to keep the end tackle from dragging at once into some underwater obstruction. Even lowering the tackle down is hazardous, and instant 'hang-ups' are commonplace. Luckily, this didn't happen to me, although several other anglers were slow on lift off and lost their tackle. Within seconds of lifting I had a typical rat-tat-tat-thump of a cod bite. Somewhere deep down my pirk bait and mackerel-fillet bait had been snapped up by a hungry cod. To avoid both snagging and foulhooking a fish, I had replaced the standard treble pirk hook with a single well-sharpened size 6–0 O'Shaughnessy hook. Some anglers prefer

to retain the vicious treble but in my experience these 'Ripper' hooks are not nearly as efficient as a well-sharpened single hook. I waited for the fish to pull the rod tip down and set the hook solidly by lifting the rod tip. Minutes later in came a splendid example of a red cod, the only such cod caught. Never common, red cod invariably come from areas where red seaweed abounds. Unlike the normally yellow-brown cod, these fish are brilliantly coloured, almost like a huge goldfish.

Well pleased with my catch, I quickly rebaited with a fresh mackerel fillet. The original fillet still looked good, but I subscribe to the view that a bait which has caught one fish seldom catches another. The theory is that a hooked fish impregnates a bait with the odour of fear or panic. Judging by the bent rods and overall activity around me, it was obvious that we had drifted over a heavy concentration of fish. Once I had a bait back at fish level it was again instant action. Nothing big, just a satisfying stream of plump cod and codling ranging from 4 lb (1.8 kg) to around 12 lb (5.4 kg). Mixed in with these was a smattering of small ling and the occasional coalfish of 2–4 lb (0.9–1.8 kg). Half a dozen times that day we drifted 'off' the fish pack. On each occasion we motored up-tide and repositioned the boat over the productive area.

Every angler's dream. A 30 lb plus (about 13.6 kg) cod. This 34-pounder (15.5 kg) was caught near the Needles, off the Isle of Wight. The bait was double squid.

Autumn days off Orkney are at best short and times passes rapidly when fish are in abundance. Soon it was all over but not before we had caught box after box of prime little cod. What the total weight was I have no real idea but at a rough guess we had at least 1,000 lb (454 kg) of fish in the boat. For me it had been a good day. I had lost only two sets of end tackle and had caught a fish on nearly every drop down. Orkney tends to be like that – no monster cod but a good, steady stream of nice fish.

Over on the west coast of Scotland the fish tend to be more patchy, but once located a shoal can throw up a number of fish near and over the magical 20 lb (9.1 kg) mark. There was a time when the Gantocks mark in the Firth of Clyde produced large numbers of huge cod. Fish of 30 lb (13.6 kg) were common and a 40-pounder (18.1 kg) could come at any time. Unfortunately the Gantocks was a short-lived hotspot. Good for a couple of winter seasons, the mark nevertheless rapidly ran out of fish. The last time I fished the area I had just one cod bite in three days of intensive fishing.

However, further up the coast, off the Isle of Mull, the fishing has remained consistently good. Whenever I fish there I arrange my trips through Brian Swinbanks of Tobermory, who has a love of fish and an understanding of them that are both almost unique. His greatest interest is in the catching, tagging and releasing of giant skate. He also knows a great deal about the local cod hotspots; so much so that I have never had a bad day's fishing with him. I remember that on one occasion when I arrived in Tobermory for just two days' fishing, conditions were wrong but Brian reckoned to find at least one cod shoal. Scottish cod are not particularly tackle-conscious and as usual the plan was to fish a big baited pirk to attract and catch fish. In this instance big was big: a giant Norwegian pirk weighing over 2 lb (0.9 kg) baited with a large mackerel fillet.

Once out of the bay, Brian eased the boat out into rough water and switched on his echo sounder. Our destination was a sharp drop-off where the water reached a depth of around 150 ft (46 m). Cod like such places, because the wall of a drop-off gives them cover and a constant supply of fish and sand eels. Big cod are hungry beasts which require a massive daily intake of food to stay in peak condition. Tide also plays an important part in a cod shoal's feeding pattern. But once you learn just which set of tide brings the cod on feed at individual marks, sport can be almost guaranteed.

By Brian's reckoning we were about an hour early on this first mark, but providing we fished feathers we could pass the time by filling the bait boxes with coalfish and mackerel, for that day bait fish were plentiful. Both species make excellent bait and it was up to the angler to catch which he wanted by fishing different levels. (Coalfish are normally caught close to the sea bed, whereas mackerel feed mostly in mid-water and above.) When bait fishing it is easy to catch and kill far more fish than you need. To avoid this I use just three feathers.

> ## COD
>
> Cod are not pretty fish: the huge head, pot belly and tapering, cylindrical body give them an ugly look. Even so, a big cod fresh from the sea and in the very pink of condition has an attraction all its own. Cod do not rate highly as fighting fish, although their bulk and obvious strength make them difficult to pump up from any depth of water; they rarely show any spirit and are usually content to plug around right under the boat. Shore anglers probably get the best out of cod fishing, particularly when a big fish is hooked in high seas.
>
> Cod are bottom feeders, favouring fairly deep water, where they will eat anything that comes their way. They shoal in loose formation and have a tendency to swim just above a wreck but below the pollack and coalfish shoals. Many are caught on red-gill or 'Eddystone' eels but for consistent results I find it pays to fish a lure and natural bait combination.
>
> In northern waters cod are present in large numbers throughout the year. In the south, the Kent and Sussex coasts often produce vast numbers of cod and codling, but it is the Needles area, off the Isle of Wight, that produces big cod in good numbers. The average size of the cod caught there is probably greater than anywhere else in the British Isles, specimens of 20 lb (9.1 kg) being commonplace.

Apart from limiting my catch, this avoids the tangles that occur with a six-feather rig. With the tide flow right for cod fishing we switched rods, tied on the huge pirks and baited the big hooks with a whole side of mackerel or coalfish. These baits looked shark size, but a cod has a big mouth and an appetite to match it. With the giant baits almost on the sea bed we started to work the lures with long, slow sweeps of the rod, hoping that the hunting cod would see the flashing dancing lure as a partially crippled fish.

For a while nothing much happened, then Brian and his brother Duncan hit fish simultaneously. The dragging rod tips and the grunts of exertion made it clear that both had good fish on. Fortunately, I had no time to watch. Something heavy and obviously hungry bit my big bait hard. Striking was unnecessary – I simply leaned back and cranked the reel handle hard. Big cod are not fighting fish, but their sheer bulk makes them difficult to pump up. This fish was typical. It shook its head and simply used its weight to move off down tide. For a second or two it took line. Then in true cod fashion it gave up and started to spiral up to the boat. By this time the Swinbanks both had their fish in the boat. While Duncan unhooked their catch, Brian stood ready to gaff my fish. Minutes later it was in the boat. A trio of near 20-pounders (9.1 kg) was a good start to what turned into a magical catch of over 20 big cod. Only one, a chunky 23-pounder (10.4 kg), actually topped 20 lb (9.1 kg). The rest ranged between 8 lb (3.6 kg) and 19 lb (8.7 kg). A good day's cod fishing by any angler's standards and a marvellous way to start a holiday in Mull.

Scottish waters are deep and clear, making baited-lure fishing easy. By contrast, in the English Channel, where the cod run much larger, the murky waters call for different tactics. The top cod fishing in the south can be found near the Needles lighthouse, off the Isle of Wight. Anglers from all over Britain come here in pursuit of a 30 lb (13.6 kg) or even a 40 lb (18.1 kg) cod. Lymington and Keyhaven are the top cod ports in Britain, each having extensive charter-boat fleets geared to winter cod hunting. The Needles area probably produces more cod of over 30 lb (13.6 kg) each season than any other cod ground in Britain. Such fish act like a magnet to cod anglers, who fish from late October to mid February in the hope of breaking personal and even British records.

Around the Needles the tides run hard and the sea is discoloured, making pirk fishing a waste of time. This is a natural bait area where the cod hunt by scent rather than sight. Here, imported Californian squid is the best bait for the big fish. Because of the strong tides and short periods of slack water, most Isle of Wight cod fishing is done with wire line. The weight and fine diameter of wire line allow the angler to get a bait down to the bottom without using the 2–2½ lb (0.9–1.1 kg) of lead required by anglers fishing Dacron or nylon line.

Back in the mid 1960s, when wire line was only just making its debut in sea angling, I was fortunate enough to be involved in the first tests on it. Both then and now three kinds of wire line were available: single-strand stainless wire; braided wire; and a composite Monel metal wire. Each was claimed by the marketing companies to be revolutionary. In practice, each had its good and bad points. Single-strand stainless was great until it kinked, which led to an instant 'break off'. Braided wire was more supple, did not kink noticeably and was pleasant to use. Unfortunately, it had a tendency to fray. This damage normally occurred well back on the line at the point where, with the bait on the bottom, 10–20 ft (3–6.1 m) of wire was passing regularly through the tip ring. Once this fraying became evident, the entire length of line had to be replaced, at considerable cost. Monel was different. It was thicker than the other two types of wire, but it did not kink or fray. These characteristics rapidly won it favour with most south of England cod anglers.

Whatever the type of wire used, it had to be fished on a rod with a roller tip ring (well oiled). Some anglers preferred rods with a complete set of roller rings. I found this unnecessary. From its introduction, wire line became a standard part of the Isle of Wight big-cod scene. The local technique was to present one or two whole squid on a sharp 8–0 hook attached to a 6, 8 or 10 ft (1.8, 2.4 or 3 m) flowing trace made up of long-liners' nylon. This was attached by a swivel to a further 3 ft (0.9 m) of nylon which held the sliding lead link. A further swivel was then used to attach the whole rig directly to a loop crimped or twisted into the wire (see Fig. 8). The trace's breaking strain was 80–100 lb (36.2–45 kg). Heavy nylon was used in preference to nylon trace wire, since the plain nylon was tough yet supple enough to allow the squid to 'kite' about in the tide flow. To add interest for the cod, some anglers attach a big plastic or metal spoon blade 6–8 in (15–20 cm) behind the bait, while others slide a plastic squid 'Muppet' onto the trace above the hook. Both lures help to attract and catch big cod.

In the right hands a wire-line outfit can be deadly. One of the best ever Isle of Wight cod catches came on a day when five of us used wire to take 450 lb (204 kg) of cod. Not one fish was less than 20 lb (9.1 kg) and six weighed in at more than 30 lb (13.6 kg). Included in this catch was a fish that remains a personal best for me, weighing exactly 39 lb (17.7 kg). This catch came in mid December. The day was icy, but the sea was comparatively calm. The mark chosen was just 1¼ miles (2 km) off the lighthouse in around 100 ft (30 m) of water. With the exception of one shallow gully, the bottom in this area is as flat as a billiards table. Past catches had shown, however, that the marauding cod shoals used this gully as a food path. Its sides doubtless gave shelter to crab, brittlestar and small pouting, all of which feature prominently in the diet of local cod.

Once anchored, we carefully threaded a brace of nice squid onto the big single hooks, having skinned each squid carefully to fully expose the white meat. Other blocks of squid were placed in buckets of salt water to defrost. Too many anglers ruin their squid by thawing it in a bucket of harbour water. This seems to taint

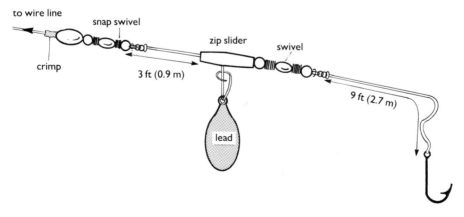

FIGURE 8   A cod leger for use with a wire line. Use a zip slider as this allows the lead to run freely between the two swivels without kinking the wire.

the bait and lessen its effectiveness. The tide had been on the run up for about an hour when we anchored. Experience has shown that the best results come on the run-up and run-off periods. Slack water is generally a waste of time for cod, although a 'hot' time for Channel whiting. As we were in the middle of a spring tide we had to use 1¼ lb (0.6 kg) of lead to keep the bait on the bottom. In wire-line fishing the trick is to get the lead size right so that it holds down until the angler lifts the rod tip and releases a few yards of line. A balanced set of terminal tackle can then be 'trotted' over the sea bed in a searching technique that can be deadly.

Other boats were also anchored in the area, one 150 yards (137 m) astern of us. Yet within minutes of starting to fish, the angler beside me had a thumping, unmissable bite which turned out to be a magnificent 26½-pounder (12 kg). This fish was quickly followed by two more 20 lb-plus (9.1 kg) fish from the opposite side of the boat. At this stage I had not even had a 'knock'. But there was certainly no shyness about the fish that day. Each had picked up the bait and slammed the rod tip hard down in the process. The scent soon washes out of a bait, and so I wound in and changed squid. This did the trick. Within five minutes I hit a big cod and after a hard tussle in came a fat 28-pounder (12.7 kg).

The average size of the fish caught so far convinced us that we were in for a magical day. The fish were bait crazy: there were none of the usual soft 'touches' that occur when cod cautiously mouth the carefully skinned squid. These fish were hungry and hit a bait accordingly. Minutes after my big cod, the angler beside me took a 34-pounder (15.4 kg). While he was playing it, two more rods slammed down, both at length yielding fish of 30 lb-plus (13.6 kg). Clearly, the first run of 20-pounders (9.1 kg) had been superseded by a batch of real monsters. To see three fish of over 30 lb (13.6 kg) in a boat on the same day is astounding, but what happened in the next hour was unbelievable.

As the last of the massive trio hit the deck, my bait was taken with a head-shaking jerk that slammed the rod down into a full fighting curve. Even big cod tend to be dour fighters, using weight rather than speed or power. This fish was different. Obviously big, it was also angry. Continuing to shake its head, it turned and ran down-tide, taking more than 30 yards (27 m) of line off against substantial drag. Despite the fact that I was using 40 lb (18.1 kg) wire, I feared that the fish would generate enough power to get round the anchor rope of the boat at our stern.

I estimated that I had over 100 yards (91 m) of line out when the cod struck, and knowing that the boat had a lot of anchor warp out my guess was that the fish was very close to snagging me. Fortunately, it did not happen. After the first run the cod slowed down and fought a slogging but not dangerous battle. Once tired, a cod tends to open its gigantic mouth, which acts as a drogue. That is exactly what this beast did. This can be a dangerous time for the angler. The intake by the fish of a large amount of water can be the final straw when the line or trace is already stretched to the limit. My luck and tackle held, and the fish came wallowing slowly up behind the boat. One quick gaff stroke and in it came. Thirty-nine pounds (17.7 kg) of magnificent cod. Not a scar, not a blemish – just a perfect fish, looking every inch its weight.

We now had 11 fish in the boat. Four of them weighed over 30 lb (13.6 kg), the rest around 25 lb (11.3 kg). What next? Having checked trace and swivels for signs of damage or fatigue I rebaited, not expecting or indeed caring to catch another fish. The Mer King wire was on my side. Within seconds I had another slamming bite and hit a second obviously big fish. This time I had no fear of the fish snagging me or an anchor cable. No cod can withstand constant rod pressure and it was not long before this one was on its way up from the bottom. Once in the boat it was swung up for weighing, and clocked in at 35¼ lb (16 kg). There was little time to admire the fish before in came the fifth 30-pounder (13.6 kg). The big fish were still under the boat and the realization that this day could produce a fish of over 40 lb (18.1 kg) affected the whole crew with cod fever.

We now had 16 fish aboard and with less than an hour to slack water, time was of the utmost importance for then the fish would instantly disperse. Again our luck held. I got a 23-pounder (10.4 kg) and three more fish hit the deck in quick time. One of these weighed 35 lb (15.9 kg). Six fish over 30 lb (13.6 kg) was unbelievable. Twenty fish in a single tide totalling 450 lb (204 kg) set a record yet to be broken in the area. As predicted, slack water totally killed the fishing. Even when the tide run started the fish did not regroup. Oddly enough, the boat anchored behind us did not take a single cod, proving that cod group in comparatively small but food-rich areas.

BEACH FISHING

It is not everyone who wants to or can afford to go boat fishing for cod. Fortunately for them, cod, even big ones, often move right inshore to feed within easy casting range of the beach. A few years ago a Welsh shore fisherman nabbed a 44-pounder (20 kg) during a night session – proof that shore fishing can be effective. The secret of shore fishing is knowing the hotspots. Years ago Dungeness beach in Kent used to be *the* place, and hundreds of anglers from all over Britain stood shoulder to shoulder just to catch a 20-pounder (9.1 kg) from the beach. In those halcyon days the 'Dungie' cod swept inshore as soon as night fell. Bites and fish were guaranteed and few anglers left the beach without a bag of cod and big whiting. But like most hotspots Dungeness finally played out. It still produces cod but in nothing like the former numbers.

The current beach hotspot is the Chesil beach in Dorset, a long bleak expanse of shingle stretching from Portland Bill to Abbotsbury. Cod do not run in huge numbers but those that do come inshore tend to be over the 20 lb (9.1 kg) mark. Like most shingle beaches Chesil is steep, and deep water can be reached by even a modest caster. Overcasting is often a mistake. Chesil cod come in close and the 150 yard-plus (137 m) caster can easily overshoot the fish-producing area. Because Chesil fish run big, most regular anglers use big baits, the two favourites being bunched lugworm and whole squid. Frozen peeler crab can also produce fish, but it is not as good as squid and worm.

Chesil is swept by strong tides, so terminal tackle has to be kept simple. A favourite rig is a one-hook paternoster fished with a spiked 'breakaway' lead. The fascination about the Chesil is its unpredictable nature: one night it will fish fantastically, while another it will totally withhold its favours. For the persever-ant angler these blank spells eventually give way to good fishing. Chesil is not the place for a one-off expedition. But when the fish do feed, the whole beach comes alive. You are just as likely to get a big spurdog or a hefty conger as a cod. The fish are there. It is just a matter of being on hand when they start to feed.

I remember one bitter night on Chesil beach at Abbotsbury. There was no real wind yet the night was icy. Several other anglers were on the beach. Lanterns gleamed and driftwood fires were very popular. Most Chesil regulars use two rods propped up in a double-headed beach rest. As normal, I followed suit, one set of tackle baited with black lug, and the other with a freshly skinned squid. I sat and watched the rod tips as they nodded to the slow suck of the tide flow. For a while there was nothing, although from the noise further along the beach it was obvious that someone had scored. Suddenly the rod baited with lugworm rattled – obviously a small pout or Channel whiting. Cursing my luck, I picked up the rod only to have it practically ripped out of my hands. Whatever it was, it was too fast for cod or conger and too big for the tackle I was using. I simply hung on to the rod as the spool of my casting reel emptied of line. Finally it was gone, leaving the line broken on the spool knot. Tope or shark, I shall never know, but this sort of thing is not uncommon on this beach. Obviously a small fish had picked up my worm bait and promptly disappeared down the gullet of something big and extremely fast.

Having neglected to pack a spare spool of line, I put this outfit away and concentrated on the remaining rod. To get one bite on Chesil is a sure indication that others will follow. Sure enough, within the hour I had a solid rat-tat at the rod tip which turned into the sort of dragging bite that is impossible to miss. By Chesil standards the resulting 10 lb (4.5 kg) cod was rather small. I didn't care, for now, with one cod on the beach, I forgot about the cold and concentrated on the fishing. Later I landed a second cod of similar size. The fish may have been small but I was pleased with the session.

FEEDING HABITS

Cod are normally bottom feeders. When cod and herring are in abundance, however, they will swim up clear of the sea bed. Cod are not selective feeders: they will eat crab, worm, shellfish, lobster, starfish and any small fish that comes within range. They are also attracted to bright-coloured objects, and many cod have been found to contain plastic cups and bright stones. This perhaps explains why a white plastic attractor spoon often brings increased catches.

TACKLE

Boat rods

The choice of rod is largely a matter of individual taste, although the area to be fished also dictates the weight and style of rod to be used. In strong tidal areas where wire line is a standard part of the equipment, a 30 or 50 lb (13.6 or 22.6 kg) class rod fitted with a quality roller tip ring is essential. The roller takes the spring out of the wire and avoids kinking. Some anglers go to the added expense of a rod which incorporates a full set of roller rings. This looks good but in terms of efficiency it achieves little. Make sure that the tip ring is kept well lubricated. A roller that does not turn can destroy a line in minutes. For fishing areas where tides are slack enough to use a nylon or Dacron line, a standard 30 lb (13.6 kg) boat rod should be sufficient. Whichever style of rod is chosen make sure that it is at least 7–7½ ft (2.1–2.3 m) in length. A short rod may cost less but it is unlikely to have the balance and power of a longer rod.

Beach rods

Most modern beach casters are made up from carbon or carbon composite (i.e. fibreglass and carbon). These materials are capable of casting a wide range of leads. In the fibreglass-only days rods were designed to throw specific weight sizes: 2–4 oz (60–115 g), 4–6 oz (115–170 g) or 6–8 oz (170–225 g). Nowadays one rod will cast leads of 4–8 oz (115–225 g), depending on conditions. For cod fishing a 12 ft (3.6 m) or even 13 ft (4 m) rod is ideal.

Reels

For boat fishing it is essential to use a multiplying reel, which should be no smaller than a Penn 4–0 or a Mitchell 624. Both are extremely good reels capable of long and faithful service. Unfortunately, however, their design has not changed in the last two decades and the discerning angler now looks to the more sophisticated lever drag reels. The best in this range are the Shimano TLD models, which are designed for specific line strengths – e.g. 15 lb (6.8 kg), 20 lb (9.1 kg), 30 lb (13.6 kg) and 50 lb (22.5 kg). This range of reels has been tried and tested all over the world and is highly regarded by both professional charter skippers and everyday anglers alike.

Lines

Nylon is probably the most widely used line material. It is tough, wears well and has an elasticity which allows it to be used and abused by anglers. The choice of brand, however, is a matter of personal preference, although very cheap nylon should always be avoided. The strain should be chosen to suit the rod being used. For boat fishing with a 30 lb (13.6 kg) class rod, use a 30 lb (13.6 kg) line. Beach casting rods are not designed for use with specific line strengths. But for all-round cod fishing an 18–20 lb (8.2–9.1 kg) line should be sufficient. Braided lines made of Dacron are no longer widely used, although for boat fishing they have an advantage over nylon in that they do not stretch under pressure. This gives more power to the strike and allows the angler to keep direct pressure on a hooked fish. The disadvantage of Dacron is that it is frayed easily by rocks or sharp shells. Once damaged, such a line may easily break without warning. Wire line is ideal for fishing strong runs of tide, allowing the angler to keep in constant

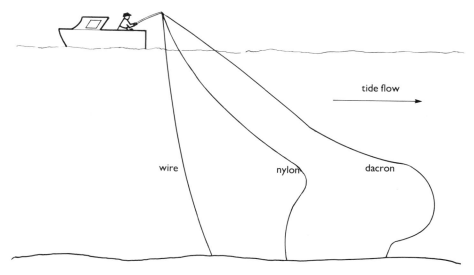

FIGURE 9 The difference in line bow between wire, nylon and Dacron. Bites registered on wire are far more definite than those on other line.

touch with the lead and terminal tackle. Both nylon and Dacron have a tendency to bow out in the tide flow, but with wire this does not occur (see Fig. 9).

TERMINAL TACKLE

Hooks

Cod are big and have huge mouths. A 14–15 lb (6.3–6.8 kg) specimen can easily swallow a 2½–3 lb (1.1–1.4 kg) whiting. Because of this it is essential to use big hooks or even two hooks. Shore anglers should use size 4–0, while boat anglers should use 6–0 or 8–0 hooks according to bait size. There is now a bewildering array of sea hooks on the market, many of the new patterns being produced in Japan and south-east Asia. These are beautifully designed and have ultra-keen chemically sharpened points. Size 4–0 hooks of this type are normally strong enough for the average shore-caught cod. But when big fish have to be fought up through deep water, and in heavy tides, such hooks are not strong enough. For this sort of fishing the tried and trusted flat forged Mustad O'Shaughnessy hook is still the best pattern to employ. But remember that these hooks are not sharp enough for immediate use, and a carborundum stone must be used to hone them.

Boat traces

At one time nylon-covered wire was necessary for cod traces. Fortunately, improved manufacturing methods in the nylon line industry have resulted in heavy-duty long-liners' nylon becoming available. This extra-tough line is perfect for making cod traces, 60 lb (27.2 kg) or 80 lb (36.2 kg) breaking strain line being the best for this purpose. At these strengths the line is still supple enough to knot, although many anglers still use a crimp beyond the knot (see Fig. 10). Such traces can be used many times and, unlike nylon-covered wire, they do not rust internally, kink or fray. A trace for use with a squid bait should be made up with a 6–0 or 8–0 hook and a sliding size 2–0 hook (see Fig. 11). The squid can then be threaded onto the big hook and held in place by the small hook (see Fig. 12). For shore work a 50 lb (22.6 kg) nylon trace incorporating a single hook is ideal.

Many anglers purchase the best rods, reels and lines available, only to spoil the entire outfit by using cheap swivels. This can be a costly mistake, for cheap swivels invariably break on big fish or may disintegrate during casting, possibly causing a serious accident. The best patterns to use are the Berkley barrel swivels which come in tested British Standard sizes. It is best to use the black swivel patterns, since the silver variety often attract pout and whiting, leading to false bites.

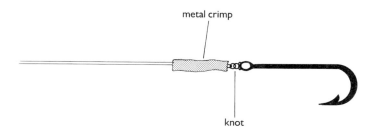

FIGURE 10   Crimped and knotted heavy-duty nylon.

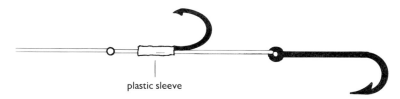

FIGURE 11   A two-hook cod rig.

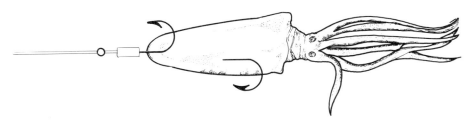

FIGURE 12   Hooking a whole squid. The finest cod bait available is white Californian squid. This is imported and sold in 5 lb (2.3 kg) packs.

METHODS

For general bottom fishing from a boat a standard running leger is the best terminal rig. This should be made up as follows (see Fig. 13). The trace itself is 6–9 ft (1.8–2.7 m) in length, and can include an attractor spoon set 8–10 in (20–25 cm) from the hook. The trace is then joined by a swivel to a further 3 ft (0.9 m) of nylon with an Ashpole or similar sliding lead boom on it. A further swivel is then used to join the entire terminal trace to the reel line. To many anglers this trace might seem over-long. The reason for its length is simple: cod like a bait that moves attractively with the tide flow, but a bait anchored on a short trace cannot 'swim' in this fashion. For shore fishing or boat fishing in

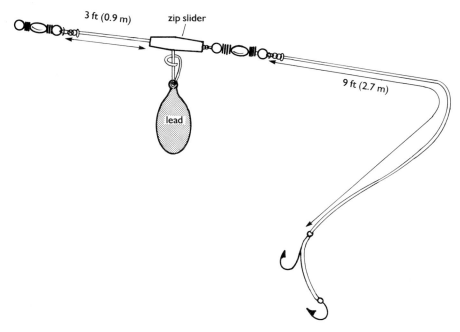

FIGURE 13   A cod leger rig. Use a zip slider and a length of nylon to allow the lead movement.

areas where cod are numerous and smallish, a simple nylon paternoster is the best rig. This is ideal for use with worm or squid/fish-strip baits.

Pirk-style baits

Originally designed by Scandinavian commercial fishermen, the pirk bait can be deadly for wreck or clear-water cod fishing. At its crudest a pirk is simply a length of chrome pipe filled at either end with lead. A wire loop is moulded into the lead, and to these loops are attached a pair of stainless split rings. One takes the hook, the other the heavy nylon trace. Tackle shops sell much more sophisticated and expensive pirk patterns, but they are no better as fish catchers than the lead-filled chrome pipe. With average DIY skills you can easily knock up a selection of pirks from old chrome piping, molten lead and heavy brass wire. But take care with the molten lead, as it is highly dangerous.

A new plastic pirk is now being marketed which comes in two halves. Special leads are sold to go with each pirk, and are added or subtracted according to the weight required. The two halves are held together by heavy rubber bands. These inexpensive plastic pirks come in bright fluorescent colours and are perfect for cod in deep water.

33

3

Conger

A medium-sized conger looks every inch its weight, but an eel of over, say, 70 lb (31.8 kg) looks like a monster. Nowadays, most of the giant conger are boat-caught fish lured from the tangled ironwork of wrecked ships. But there was a time when some huge eels still lurked round various West Country harbours and estuary walls. The majority of such fish have long since died or been caught. Even so, there is still the occasional fish of 50 lb (22.6 kg), 60 lb (27.2 kg) or even 70 lb (31.8 kg), and often such fish are known as individuals. Many have been hooked and lost on a score of occasions; when a huge conger makes its last mistake its mouth will be seen to contain the rusting remains of hooks and traces; mementoes of old battles that have made the fish a legend in its own life time.

Unlike most fish, which feed and move on, the conger is a residential species. It is a slimy, grey-black marauder that emerges under cover of darkness to raid and scavenge until daylight sends it slithering back into some sea-worn hole in the harbour wall. Inshore conger are essentially night feeders. Offshore, over deep wrecks, the fish live in perpetual darkness, feeding with the changing tides rather than the onset of night.

HARBOUR FISHING

Some of my most memorable conger fishing has taken place in West Country harbours. Mevagissey, in Cornwall, has always been a firm favourite of mine. Harbour fishing is mostly a summer and autumn occupation. Because of holiday crowds, serious fishing is rarely possible before 9 or 10 at night. By this time the quays are clear of aimless humanity and fishing can begin in earnest. Harbour conger fishing is relatively straightforward. The fishing position is a safe one and the fish are usually found round the base of the harbour walls, which makes for comfortable fishing and easy casting. The drawback, however, is that any conger that does pick up the bait is within a short distance of its home. Under these conditions light tackle is useless, for a biting eel has to be struck and stopped almost instantly.

Tackle

The ideal rig is an 11 or 12 ft (3.3 or 3.6 m) casting rod and a multiplying reel loaded with 35 lb (15.9 kg) or even 40 lb (18.1 kg) nylon line. The rod should be capable of casting leads of 8–10 oz (225–285 g). Terminal tackle is very basic: a running boom slid directly on the reel line, a single large barrel swivel and no more than 3 ft (0.9 m) of 100 lb (45 kg) breaking strain nylon for the trace. Wire is not recommended, since particularly in the heavier breaking strains it is stiff and inclined to alarm a feeding eel. The hook should be a well-sharpened 8–0 or 10–0 O'Shaughnessy or Mustad Seamaster pattern. Cheap hooks are an abomination, often straightening or snapping under pressure.

For inshore conger the best bait is fish. Conger hunt by scent and a freshly cut fish oozing blood and body juices will tempt even the most well fed of eels. All anglers have their preferred bait fish. Mackerel, having an oiliness that is very attractive to conger, seems to top the list, but pollack, pouting, horse mackerel (sead) and wrasse are all good baits. A bag of supermarket sardines also takes a lot of beating. These are soft and easily broken up, but their oily flesh is a powerful attractant. Whatever the bait, it must be fresh. Conger may be classed as scavengers, but given the choice of fresh or stale bait the fresh will produce the goods whereas the stale may fail miserably.

I recall one Cornish night session when I spent the last hour of daylight catching large horse mackerel for bait. At nightfall I changed my light tackle for the heavy conger gear described above and headed back to the end of the quay to meet a fishing friend. Conger are difficult fish to land and it pays to fish in company. Fortunately, Tony was a keen conger angler. Over a number of seasons he had notched up an impressive list of 'snakes' including a 60-pounder (27.2 kg) taken from the Braye harbour breakwater in Alderney. We had fished together many times before and the present session was a carefully planned trip to a quay which had produced some hefty conger in its day. By the time I had walked out to the quay head Tony was already fishing. His rod was propped up by a low tripod, with the heavy line slanting sharply down into darkness. With my tackle already made up it was the work of seconds to split the head of a good-sized horse mackerel and pass the hook through its body about 4 in (10 cm) back from the tail. I like to fish a bait cut in this way. The head and gills hold a lot of blood and send off a good, strong scent. Any conger crossing this smell lane will normally follow it back to its source and pick the bait up. Tony was fishing a half mackerel. Cut through the middle, the oily flesh gives off a good oil slick.

Conger can reach weights in excess of 100 lb (45 kg). This 60 lb (27.2 kg) specimen is in peak condition. Most eels of this size are taken from wreck marks. This monster swallowed up a bait intended for cod.

CONGER

A timid creature which retreats at the slightest sign of danger, a big conger eel is nevertheless the most powerful fish any sea angler can expect to encounter off the British coast. The strength of a hooked conger is prodigious, and it takes a strong and fit angler to deal with a really large specimen. Very big conger are regarded by most sea anglers as an offshore species, and deep-water wrecks are where most big eels are caught.

A monster conger weighing 180 lb (81.5 kg) was washed ashore on the French coast in 1961; another, of 142 lb (64 kg), turned up on Walcott Beach, Norfolk, in 1956; and another, weighing 96 lb (43.5 kg), was found barely alive at Minehead in Somerset in 1959. Two other giant specimens have also been found: one, of 90 lb (40.7 kg), was washed up at Portland in Dorset in 1956; the other, of 86 lb (38.9 kg), was washed up in the Orwell Estuary, Suffolk, in 1961. Finally, an eel weighing 84 lb (38 kg) was washed ashore on the North Yorkshire coast in 1957 and an 87 lb (39.4 kg) specimen was caught by hand on the North Wales coast in 1959. This last fish had been left behind by the retreating tide and was very much alive at the time it was found.

In my view these figures provide material proof of the existence of very big conger in inshore waters. I would strongly advise keen conger anglers to survey thoroughly the likely marks close to the shore before pinning their hopes on distant, deep-water grounds. I suspect that conger which live in areas where no one suspects their presence eventually die of old age or become too feeble to feed themselves properly, and so drift ashore, either as fresh corpses or in a severely weakened condition.

Most anglers now assume that to catch a monster eel it is essential to go wreck fishing. Records show that this is far from true, for many huge conger have been taken in relatively shallow water. Numerous specimens of between 80 and 100 lb (36.2–45 kg) have been recorded. The weights listed above suggest that conger can exceed 200 lb (91 kg), although eels of over 100 lb (45 kg) are still rare, mainly because such fish are rarely hooked far from cover and so have no trouble smashing tackle.

Conger can be caught at almost any time of year, but the late summer and autumn months usually fish the best. It is a popular fallacy that conger are 'dirty' feeders living mainly on rotten fish gleaned from the sea bed. This idea is nonsense. As a general rule, conger are much less inclined than skate or ray to eat stale food. Although I have caught conger on a stinking bait, I have always found stale baits to be inferior to fresh ones when this species is the quarry.

Distance casting with a big bait and a 40 lb (18.1 kg) line is out of the question. Fortunately, it is also unnecessary, for most harbour conger are caught within 30 yards (27 m) of the stonework. With this in mind I lobbed the big bait and 4 oz (115 g) weight out, and settled the rod into its tripod. I clicked the ratchet button into the 'on' position, tightened up the line and pulled back the spool-release lever. The ratchet tension was enough to withstand the tide pull but would give line the instant an eel pulled the bait. From ten until nearly midnight, nothing happened. A bait check produced a large starfish. These pests can maul a bait and once this happens conger normally refuse to touch it. I split and attached a new bait, recast and settled back. Big conger can be extremely gentle feeders. In fact the larger the eel the lighter the bite. Small 'whips' of up to 10 or 12 lb (4.5 or 5.4 kg) really tear into a bait. A big conger is very different: often the only warning is a gentle pulling at the rod tip.

On this occasion my reel gave a single click. Instantly, I had the rod in my hand and pushed the ratchet knob into the 'off' position. With a thumb on the reel spool I could feel the eel through the line – nothing hittable, just the occasional pluck as it mouthed the bait. After several minutes of this the eel seemed to make up its mind that the bait was acceptable. Almost imperceptibly the line began to tighten and the reel spool to turn. Manually pulling a yard of line off the reel, I slipped the reel into gear, and waited as the loose line pulled tight. Then, as the weight of the fish started to pull the rod tip down I struck, cranked in the slack, and struck again, grinding the reel handle round to gain line. For a second everything felt solid. Then the eel made its plunging rush for whatever stone cavity it called home.

This is when the heavy tackle comes into its own. Light gear would have been smashed by the power of a newly hooked eel, but the heavy line allowed me to use the hefty rod as a lever. The outcome of a battle with a conger is decided in the first vital seconds. Get the eel up and flustered and you have every chance of bringing the fight to a satisfactory conclusion. Give an inch and the eel will be home and safely wedged in its stronghold. Once this happens, it's goodbye eel: nothing will induce it to give ground. As usual, instant brute force stopped the eel in its tracks. This gave me time to move along the quay wall while at the same time I got the fish up a few valuable feet off the bottom. Once prised away from their sanctuary, conger often become flustered. It would seem that they have only one strategy. When this fails they panic, making short runs in all directions as if probing desperately for some hole or obstruction to slide under. This haphazard way of fighting normally ends when the eel starts to spin.

Spinning seems to be the eel's last resort and can be very dangerous, for a rusted and seized-up swivel will often part under this brutal treatment and inferior hooks simply bend or snap. Fortunately, my terminal gear was new and well cared for. When my eel finally resorted to spinning it was already round the quay head on its way into the steps and a waiting gaff. One of the beauties of fishing West Country harbours is that you can nearly always stand directly above the gaffman, so that you can drag the hooked conger straight in. The gaffman can then sink the gaff in point uppermost. As you pull the eel over the gaff the gaffman can drive the point solidly home. Tony did just that, and seconds later he was bounding up the steps dragging a thrashing eel behind him. Once on the quay the eel was rapidly dispatched, unhooked, sacked and weighed by torch light. No monster, but a good eel weighing a fraction over 30 lb (13.6 kg).

When I hooked my eel Tony had naturally wound in his tackle. A crossed line or worse, two eels on at the same time, could have led to real complications. Now, as I attached a fresh trace and bait, Tony was again fishing. Seconds later he was into a fish. It is surprising how often you catch one conger and others follow. Whether vibrations set up by a struggling eel cause others to investigate I do not know, but once a conger has been taken the local eel community goes on a feeding spree. As it turned out, this eel was a little 'strap' which looked like it weighed less than 10 lb (4.5 kg). The hook was clearly visible in the corner of its jaw. A seconds work with a home made 'T' bar (see Fig. 14) removed the hook, and the eel went back in the water. Even the prolific conger needs conserving, and I hoped that this one would grow on to provide sport in future seasons. From midnight to first light we took four more eels: one keepable at 25 lb (11.3 kg), the rest returnable. Once dawn starts to show, conger normally retire to their caves and crevices. Very much a nocturnal species, most shallow-water conger refuse to feed in daylight, except in coloured water. Even then their daytime forays are normally brief.

'T' bar

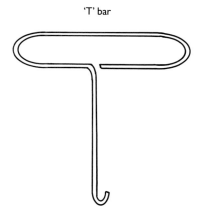

FIGURE 14 A 'T' bar is useful for hooking conger. It can also be used for cod and ling.

ESTUARY FISHING

Like many other sea fish, conger like an inflow of fresh water.

A typical estuary stronghold for conger is the disued china-clay jetties on Cornwall's Fowey river. The resident eels provide some 'hot' fishing for any angler willing to risk a lot of terminal tackle among the many snags adjacent to the jetty foundations. I have always fished the Fowey hotspots with top West Country skipper John Affleck. For many years John lived on the Fowey at Golant, and his knowledge of the river and its big fish were second to none. It was he who introduced me to the local conger hotspots. I was in Cornwall for a few days' wreck fishing, but as it turned out I got just one day out before the wind changed, making it impossible to leave Fowey harbour. Beyond Gribbin Head the sea was foaming, great foam-tipped peaks of solid green water. John said that wrecking was out of the question but that he knew another place where we could get some good conger. Our first stop was the fish shop at Par to pick up mackerel as bait. The second stop was the local garage to find enough spark plugs to make expendable weights. I did not have any heavy beach-casting tackle with me. John advised me to use a 30 lb (13.6 kg) class boat rod and a reel to match – hardly shore-fishing tackle but we had no choice.

By 10 pm the wind was still howling through the streets but we decided to go ahead and fish anyway, for conditions are seldom perfect. At night the totally deserted and in some cases ruined quays had a strange, brooding atmosphere. Below, the wind-ruffled river ran past like black treacle. Despite the fierce wind the air temperatures were high and we had hopes of success. A warm night, a rising tide and comparatively warm sea temperatures usually put conger in a good feeding mood. The short, heavy rods were hardly appropriate, but they worked to the tune of eight conger weighing between 17 lb (7.7 kg) and 36 lb (16.3 kg). Two other huge fish were lost. Both were played for long, anxious minutes only to turn and dive back into a solid obstruction. The water was only 15–20 ft (4.6–6 m) deep, so the bottom was at most only a few feet beneath the hooked fish. In the past these old china-clay jetties have produced several eels of over 50 lb (22.6 kg), and both of the lost fish felt as if they were around that weight. An intensive session on the Fowey might well produce some big surprises.

SHALLOW-WATER CONGER

Conger are normally found near rocks, rugged water-worn stonework or other solid obstructions. But this is not always the case. On the Solent marshes, in what is usually regarded as smooth-hound and stingray territory, conger often live in shallow water, using sea-dug holes as shelter. In this area the sedge or marsh is semi-solid, falling directly into gullies or shallow drop-offs. Providing the drop-off does not dry out at low tide, it will almost certainly hold a few eels. No monsters, but fish up to about 15 lb (6.8 kg), which provide plenty of sport on standard beach-casting tackle. Conger are probably far more common over inshore marks than most anglers realize. I have caught them from the Kyle of Lochalsh to the Scilly Islands. Few anglers shore fish for them, but if more did I am certain some interesting catches would occur. The big freeze of 1962–3 killed off thousands of conger of all sizes. Some of these big losses occurred in areas where no one realized there was a conger population. At that time thousands of eels were washed ashore, some of them monsters of over 100 lb (45 kg).

Most of the really big rod-caught eels have been offshore fish. Without exception, every eel of over 90 lb (40.8 kg) was a wreck fish. This does not mean that it is impossible to catch a big eel from inshore waters. But it does indicate that shore and inshore anglers simply do not gear up for really big eels. Therefore when one does come along it invariably breaks free, sometimes without the angler even realizing he has hooked a giant conger. Many an inshore angler has had a good bite and struck at a moving fish, only to find everything go solid. After the usual heaving and pulling, the line parts and the angler puts it down to a snag. When stories like this begin to circulate they often attract the attention of a few top anglers. The result is that giant eels are weighed in; fish that have come from areas regarded as devoid of conger.

South-west Ireland is a great place for conger, the rugged coastline of Co. Kerry and the many fishing harbours providing ideal haunts for eels. Whereas conger in British waters are almost exclusively nocturnal, in the less hard-fished Irish harbours eels can be caught right through the day. Ireland is very good for a boat fishing holiday, although the weather can often be bad. To avoid lost fishing time it pays to pack a hefty beach-casting outfit. Then, when the offshore fishing marks are unreachable, you can turn with confidence to harbour or rock-gulley conger fishing. Harbour conger live on fish scraps and pieces dumped from lobster and long-line boats. They are not fussy about bait, and as long as it is fairly fresh and meaty they will feed on it.

I used to fish a tiny rock-bound slipway on Slea Head, in Co. Kerry. The place was used for launching a pair of coracles. These homebuilt, tarred-canvas boats are still widely used in the south and west of Ireland. The Slea Head boats were used exclusively for lobster fishing. At the end of each day trash was simply thrown out onto the slipway. The incoming tide then washed it out into deep, rocky water. The first time I found this slipway I was on a wrasse-fishing expedition. Food, deep water and a solid rock reef bottom: just the sort of place that could yield some good eels.

The next day I was back with a heavy rig, a bag of spark plugs and a string of freshly caught mackerel. I made up the tackle as a running leger using a link swivel in place of a running boom. To the link I attached a heavy-duty rubber band, and then attached two spark plugs to the band (see Fig. 15). The hook was baited with the head end of a mackerel hooked just once through the eye sockets. Conger love fish heads (a tip I learned while working on Cornish long-line boats). Long-range casting was unnecessary so I lobbed the bait out 40 yards (37 m) and propped the rod up on a tall tripod. For a while, nothing. Then the rod tip nodded as a questioning eel pulled at the juicy bait. I picked up the rod and lowered the tip a few inches to give the eel some slack line. Instantly it was off with the bait. This first Slea Head eel virtually hooked itself. Seconds later it snagged the spark plugs in the rocks. I knew it was the weights, for I could still feel the eel pulling hard. This was where the rubber band came into its own. As the pressure increased the band snapped leaving the eel to fight on a weight-free line. I learned this trick while wrasse fishing with Alderney maestro Roddy Hayes. To the uninitiated the band and spark plugs set-up may look like a gimmick, but it can save endless sets of terminal tackle and more than a few fish.

Once free of the snag, the eel was easy to play out. At about 12 lb (5.4 kg) it was not keepable. The hook was in the corner of its mouth. By using a 'T' bar I was able to shake the fish off the hook and drop it back into the foam. After a quick check of the trace and hook and fitting a new rubber band, I was back in business. In all I had 11 conger ranging from 8 lb (3.6 kg) to 18 lb (8.2 kg). All but the largest I returned. This I kept for one of the coracle men. During the session I lost many spark plugs, one hook, and a dozen or so rubber bands. But had I used shop-bought leads and booms it would have been a costly day's sport.

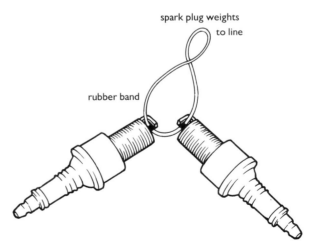

FIGURE 15 Spark plug weights prevent expensive leads being lost. For conger use a rubber band to join two plugs to the line.

42

BOAT FISHING

The best-ever inshore boat fishing trip I can remember was off Brook ledges on the Isle of Wight. The ground in this area is made up of peaks and ledges fissured by deep, narrow cracks – ideal territory for a multitude of conger. July and August tends to be the time to fish Brook, and a rising tide with no moon provides the perfect conditions. Under these circumstances air and water temperatures are high and the local conger go on a feeding spree that is hard to match. These conditions have given me many good nights on Brook, but one stands out from all the rest.

Reaching Brook at 9 pm, with just about an hour to go before dark, we stopped short of the extensive ledges to feather two boxes of bait mackerel. It seemed enough at the time but later I wished we had thought to catch more. With plenty of light to pick out shore marks we set the anchor in about 40 ft (12 m) of water. The echo sounder showed we were in a gully surrounded by walls of vertical rock. Brook ledges are swept by heavy tides. Even neap tides can be strong here, and so we had brought along several buckets of assorted leads. As always the end tackle consisted of a simple running leger and 100 lb (45 kg) breaking strain wire trace. Long-liners' nylon is now used in preference to the rather stiff wire, but at that time it was not readily available. End-tackle losses were expected to be high and the six anglers aboard had made up enough traces to last the night.

On arriving at slack water we had chopped up a dozen prime mackerel and dropped them over the side. By twilight we were all baited up and ready to go, expecting to catch conger and bull huss. Brook is one of those areas that often produce a few surprises. The trip was an 'invitational', all the anglers having been chosen for their ability. One of our top rods was Carlo, an Italian long-time resident in Britain. It was going to be his night, although at that time none of us knew it. As darkness increased I had a strong pull of a bite which turned out to be a 16 lb (7.3 kg) bull huss. Two more of similar size were soon boated but as yet there was no sign of the conger.

Twenty, thirty, forty minutes passed with nothing else to show for our efforts. Suddenly, my rod was almost ripped out of my hands by something that tore off down-tide at high speed. Five minutes later it was still fighting hard. A tope, I thought, yet that seemed unlikely for I had never caught or heard of a tope being caught at night or from such a rugged piece of ground. A tope it was, however, and a big one. It was not weighed but was estimated to be around 40 lb (18.1 kg) before being released. Shortly after, the conger came on the feed. Not just the odd fish, but waves of them. At times it seemed that everyone on the boat was into a fish at the same time. In fact, I stopped fishing and became gaffman. As each conger was swung inboard I cut the trace and dropped the eel into a plastic dustbin, for conger slime can turn an already wet deck into a skating rink. The dustbins kept both the decks clean and the eels quiet.

By 1 am I was onto the last and fifth dustbin and still the eels kept coming. Most were on the big side, stocky fish in the 25–30 lb (11.3–13.6 kg) class with the odd 40-pounder (18.1 kg) thrown in. It is amazing how many eels a dustbin can hold. They pack themselves in nose to tail and never move again. By my estimate we had close to 1,000 lb (454 kg) of eels in the boat and the fishing was still hot. Carlo, who had been doing better than most, suddenly let out a grunt. When I reached him his rod was doubled over as somewhere below us a very big eel fought a vicious battle for its freedom. Suddenly it started to swim up and as its head broke surface I struck with the gaff and heaved it inboard.

It went berserk, tore off the gaff and fell writhing and slapping against the dustbins. So great was its strength, it sent the dustbins flying, dumping a mass of live eels on the deck. One minute I was operating on a clean and tidy boat, the next I seemed to be up to my knees in angry, slimy eels. No sooner did I get a dustbin half full of eels than it was knocked over again. Finally, I had to use a special forked eel knife to chop through the spine of each eel.

Last back into the bin was Carlo's monster. It was clearly over 50 lb (22.6 kg) and I was anxious to see it weighed. With the decks clear, all hands got to work with brush and deck hose. Once it was safe to walk about we swung the big eel up on the scales where it swung the pointer to 58 lb (26.3 kg). Everyone was anxious to start again, but it was only an hour until dawn and as it turned out the conger had just about finished feeding. We got a couple more before Carlo was suddenly back in action. At first the fish fought hard: a dashing, different sort of battle that kept us guessing. But in the end the strong conger tackle wore it down and as it surfaced I was amazed to see a 12½ lb (5.7 kg) bass on the line. How a normally finicky fish like a big bass came to pick up half a mackerel on 100 lb (45 kg) trace wire I shall never know. But it did and I could see that Carlo was delighted. What a night! More conger than we could have imagined plus a tope and a monster bass.

WRECK FISHING

Many anglers would argue that such a catch is insignificant compared with big wreck hauls. This may be so in terms of weight and size but not in terms of fun. Wreck conger are normally hooked at anywhere from 35 to 50 fathoms (64–91 m). Sometimes even more. In its heyday, in the late 1970s, wreck fishing regularly produced eels of 80–100 lb (36.2–45 kg). The present record eel, weighing 109 lb (49 kg), is a monster by any standards, but much bigger eels were fought and lost at that time. Unfortunately, such fish were normally taken on 80 lb (36.2 kg) line and fencing-wire traces. Once such a tackle became snagged, most of the lost monsters died tethered to the very wreckage that had once been their home. How many giant conger died in this way there is no way of knowing, but it is now rare for anyone to boat an eel of over 80 lb (36.2 kg). Yet wreck fishing for conger remains an exciting sport.

The occasional eel snatches at a drift-fished bait, but most conger are caught at anchor. Anchoring a wreck is a very skilled operation. The skipper has to take into account tide speeds, depth of water and many other critical factors. The aim is to fish up-tide of the wreck so that the baits can be rolled back into its base. If the sunken ship lies across the normal tide flow it is fairly easy to anchor correctly. Unfortunately, however, few ships sank to order. Most offshore wrecks are the victims of two wars. Most were sunk by torpedo or by bombs dropped from the air. The force of the explosion caused most sunken ships to go down at an angle, so each has to be approached as a separate problem. A good wreck skipper has a fairly accurate mental picture of the layout of each of the wrecks he knows. This allows him to give his anglers the best chance of getting their baits in to where the big eels are likely to be lurking.

Wreck-fishing tackle

At its best wreck fishing for conger is a rough and rugged sport. Experienced anglers use 80 lb (36.2 kg) class gear with size 6–0 or 9–0 reels. Nylon is regarded as the best reel line even though its elasticity can lead to lost fish. Dacron is frowned upon. Braided lines may not stretch but they do fray, and contact with a sea-worn, rusted piece of steel can lead to an instant breakage. Wire lines are also regarded as a menace. In the early days of wrecking, wire was used because it cut through the tide. Certainly it produced several eels between 80 and 100 lb (36.2 and 45 kg). The problem lay not in its reliability but in its danger: once snagged up the wire had to be broken out by hand, and heavy wire line can cut like a cheese wire. For this reason it is not recommended for wrecking.

To catch eels you must know when your baited end tackle touches bottom and then be able to trot it back to the wreck. Some anglers have difficulty in feeling the initial bump of the lead on the sea bed. If this is not felt and the line checked it is easy to carry on releasing line. Doing so creates a line bow which will ultimately build up sufficient water pressure to lift the lead and bait clear of the sea bed. This invariably ends in a bad tangle or the snagging of the terminal rig. Once bottom is felt the line should be stopped by clamping the thumb down on the reel spool. The rod tip should then be lifted and line released until the lead touches down again. This action can be repeated a number of times to trot the baited tackle into the wreck itself. Once the wreck is reached the thump of the lead has a different feel to it. At this stage the reel should be locked up ready for instant action.

Wreck conger seldom mess around with a bait, for they are in constant, fierce competition with other eels. Food which is brought to them on the tide flow is seen as natural and taken accordingly. The first bite is normally indicated by a solid thump on the rod tip. A good trick is to slowly wind in a yard (metre) or two of line. This will get the eel out of its hole and give you a chance to force it out into open water. A bait which moves away from a hungry conger is normally taken with a savage bang. At the same instant the conger will turn for home. An experienced wreck angler will strike, heave and wind in all at the same time. Fluster a big eel into open water and you have every chance of getting it into the boat. Fail to bully it and it will dive deep into the wreckage. Once inside, there is little hope of bringing it out again.

Deep-water wreck conger cannot be fought like other species. It is simply a matter of who is the stronger. If the angler can get the eel to move upward then he has every chance of winning the fight. Once mid water is reached the struggle is just about over. But never relax at this stage, for conger are quick to sense a tactical advantage. Highly adept at the last-minute crash dive, a conger can only be regarded as caught when it drops into the fish hold. Practically every wreck-boat skipper tells his own version of the story of the lost monster conger, relating how monster eels were brought to the surface and even in some cases gagged. In all these stories there is one constant factor: a second's lapse of concentration by the angler or skipper. Many of these lost monsters have smashed gaff handles, lines and even rods and vanished back into the depths forever.

I remember one such beast. We were scheduled to fish the almost complete wreck of a torpedoed freighter. The wreck dated from World War 2 and was in 40 fathoms (73 m) of water 30 miles (48 km) off the Dorset coast. We had already spent four days over the wreck catching several thousands pounds of pollack and ling on baited pirks and artificial sand eels. To get a bait down to conger level it is essential to 'clear' the wreck first. After four days of hard but productive fishing we were sure we could now get big baits down without them being constantly intercepted by ever-hungry ling. Bait was no problem and by the time we were anchored to fish the wreck we had boxes of plump Dorset mackerel stacked up ready for use.

This was the last day of a five-day trip planned to coincide with the slackest of neap tides. Once the tide was at full flow we had little chance of fishing. Now we had an hour of slackening tide and nearly an hour of slack water, plus what time we could glean once the tide started to pick up again. At best we had 2¼ hours of fishing ahead – time enough to lift a big catch of conger out of the rusting freighter. The first fish aboard was a monster pout. How this 3½ lb (1.6 kg) nuisance had managed to eat half a mackerel on a 10–0 hook remains a mystery.

But I did know that pout is a top conger bait. I quickly wound in, changed to a pout head with the guts left dangling (see Fig. 16) and quickly got into a good eel. Conger love fresh pout and the blood and body juices of a newly caught pout will draw them like a magnet. This eel weighed over 40 lb (18.1 kg) but well under 50 lb (22.6 kg). A good fish to start with.

The ever-slackening tide brought the eels out on a food hunt. Right up to the middle part of slack water they fed solidly. Disappointingly, they were all medium-sized by wreck standards. The best looked about 50 lb (22.6 kg) or more, the smallest about half that weight. Without warning, bites ceased. The tide was still perfect so it seemed likely that a large predator was working the wreck. The skipper surmised that it was probably a stray porbeagle, and I was inclined to agree with him. Shark often raid wrecks. Pollack and ling are their main targets, but they will also take conger when the opportunity arises.

After 10–15 minutes without a bite we were all cursing the 'shark' for spoiling our sport, when the angler closest to the wheelhouse let out a gasp. Turning, I could see his rod forming an incredible hoop. I thought, mistakenly, that he was hung up on the wreck. A wreck is static, but whatever he was hooked to was not. Each time it shook its head both the rod and the angler lurched in unison. Fortunately, he was using heavy gear. His rod was an old-fashioned solid fibreglass affair which looked capable of stopping a battleship. The reel was a 9–0 Penn Senator fully loaded with heavy nylon. Obviously shaken by the power of the fish, the angler nevertheless stood the strain well. Using the pump-and-wind-down technique he was slowly but surely gaining ground. The 'shark', for that is what we believed it to be, was on its way up. My fear was that his 3 ft (0.9 m) foot trace was far too short. Should even tough nylon come into contact with a shark's abrasive skin it will chafe through in seconds.

Somehow everything held, and with all our baits inboard we gathered to watch the struggle. By this time the angler had regained his confidence. The fish was lifting, 'kiting' slowly up and doing little more than shake its head. At the mid-water mark it attempted to dive, taking a few yards of easily retrievable line. A medium-sized porbeagle, was the general consensus of opinion. Judging by the build-up of line on the reel it would soon be in sight. Finally, far down, a glimmer of grey showed. 'Definitely a shark', someone said. I was not sure. From what I had seen the fish was long but too lean to be a porbeagle. It looked to me like a monster of a conger. A little nearer and we could see it clearly: it was an eel of unbelievable size, with a huge broad head and a back like a pig's. What its weight was I could not guess. I had seen several 100-pounders (45 kg) but this eel looked even bigger.

At this stage the eel was coming up quietly, allowing itself to be led like a dog on a lead. It was either very tired or about to go totally berserk. It chose the latter course, and as the skipper leaned out with the gaff it went into the last-ditch

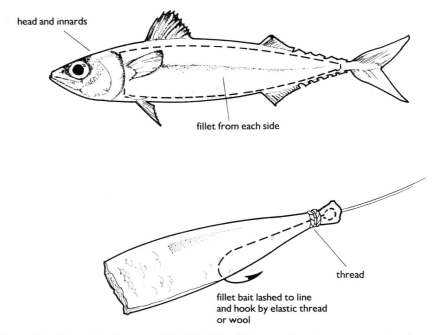

head and innards

fillet from each side

thread

fillet bait lashed to line
and hook by elastic thread
or wool

FIGURE 16   Three baits from one fish. Oily-fleshed baits are often best as conger hunt by
scent as much as by sight. Try mackerel, pilchard or herring.

rolling spin characteristic of all the conger tribe. The gaff missed it completely
and almost at the same time the tackle flew back out of the water. Like a flash the
eel vanished in a running dive that left a vortex on the calm surface. The hook
was snapped – not surprising, because it was one of those American-style
beaked hooks which look so good but break so easily under strain. Had the
angler used a solid forged O'Shaughnessy or a cadmium-plated Mustad Seamaster that eel would have ended its life on deck. Now it was back in its retreat
with a sore lip to remember us by.

Once again it had been proved that no matter how good and how costly your
rod, reel, and line, it is the hook that takes the strain. With the right hook the
conger record could have toppled. That wreck has been fished many times since,
but not once has the big eel been contacted. Maybe it died. More likely it learned
its lesson and has shunned everything but live fish ever since.

TACKLE

Conger are bottom feeders normally found over the roughest underwater terrains. There have been attempts, mostly unsuccessful, at using light tackle for conger. Most experienced conger anglers select heavy gear.

Boat rods

For general rough-ground fishing a 50 lb (22.6 kg) class rod is more than adequate. For wrecking, however, an 80 lb (36.2 kg) class rod is more suitable. A perfect compromise is the new Shimano Beastmaster (50–130 lb/22.6–59 kg class). This is an ultra-powerful one-piece rod designed to tame huge big-game fish. It is built from a single carbon blank and weighs less than most 30 lb (13.6 kg) class boat rods. Designed as a 'stand-up' rod, the Beastmaster is perfect for use with a butt pad.

Beach casters

For shore and harbour fishing it is essential to choose your rod carefully. Many carbon and fibreglass patterns make long casting simple. However, a rod may look fantastic in the tackle shop, but on the beach prove to be an expensive disaster. It is best to buy a rod from a known maker who gives a reasonable guarantee. Also, take the rod apart and check the wall thickness of the blank. Some rods are of paper-thin construction, and totally useless for the rigours of conger fishing. If you can afford it, go to a specialist rod builder and together devise a specification that suits all your requirements.

Shore reels

The only reel that can be used for shore conger fishing is a medium-sized shore-fishing multiplier. Fixed-spool reels may be easier to cast with but the first big eel will certainly wreck the bale mechanism. Many good multipliers are available. For example, the Leeda 624, the Penn 4–0, and the Shimano TLD 20 are all capable of holding 150 yards (137 m) or more of 35–40 lb (15.9–18.1 kg) breaking strain line.

Boat reels

Again, only the best will do. The ideal choice is the Shimano TLD 25. Tried and tested against some of the world's top fish, it has a magnificent lever-drag system which allows the angler to apply maximum pressure without fear of a breakage.

The Penn 6–0 Senator is another excellent reel for heavy-duty use, and is particularly suitable for wreck fishing.

Lines

For fishing moderate depths and hard tides wire line can be used to catch conger. For this sort of fishing a single-strand wire with a breaking strain of 40–50 lb (18.1–22.6 kg) is recommended. For all other forms of conger fishing nylon line is best.

Traces

Heavy-duty long-liners' nylon with a breaking strain of 100 lb (45 kg) or more is the perfect trace material. Supple and yet hard, it can be knotted and then crimped (see Fig. 10) for maximum security.

Swivels

Hooked conger usually spin violently in an attempt to shake free of the hook. To overcome this tackle-twisting motion top-quality swivels should be used. The best and most expensive are the Sampo swivels. Less costly but just as effective are the Berkley swivels from the USA.

Hooks

Only the best hooks will do for conger fishing, and this means Mustad Seamasters and O'Shaughnessy patterns. The sizes to use are 6–0, 8–0, and 10–0. Shakespeare also produces an extremely good conger hook, the stainless-steel Model Perfect, available in sizes up to 10–0.

4

Dogfish, Spurdog and Smooth-Hound

DOGFISH

The commonest dogfish in British waters is the diminutive lesser-spotted dog-fish, which is generally regarded as little more than a bait-robbing vermin. But at least it can often be induced to feed when all other species spurn a bait. The greater-spotted variety reaches a greater weight, making it a much more interest-ing fish to catch. Commonly known as the bull huss, it is far more nocturnal than the lesser-spotted dogfish. While lesser-spotted dogfish are normally found over flat areas of sand or shingle, the bull huss prefers a rocky bottom where during the day it rests. Under cover of darkness it cruises through submerged rock gullies in search of food. Although it is a capable hunter, the bull huss scavenges in the manner of the lesser-spotted dogfish. Both species eat fish, molluscs and crustacea.

Most bull huss are caught on cut fish, mackerel and herring being the best baits. For bull huss I like to use a fish head with the guts and gills attached (see Fig. 16). The bait should be cut three quarters of the way through. A quick pull will tear through the remainder of the body, leaving the guts intact. A head bait should be hooked once through both eye sockets. Once on the bottom the head will lay a strong, highly appealing scent trail. A huss that locks onto this will usually follow it to its source and take the bait instantly. The old nickname for the bull huss was 'bounce', a name inspired by its head-wagging way of biting which causes the rod tip to bob up and down like a bouncing ball. Most rod-caught huss weigh between 9 lb (4 kg) and 13 lb (6 kg), although commercial methods often take fish of twice the heavier weight.

DOGFISH

The bull huss is the largest of the two common dogfish. Big, greedy fish which can easily exceed 20 lb (9.1 kg), bull huss are reddish-brown, with large, dark blotches. They are commonest over rough ground, often frequenting good conger marks. Bull huss can be caught during the day, but in my experience feed best after dark. The lesser-spotted dogfish, which seldom attains any great size, lives mainly on sandy ground and makes a nuisance of itself by taking baits. It is similar in colour to the bull huss, except that its spots are small and very neat. Both fish have the unpleasant habit of wrapping themselves round an unwary hand and then slowly unwinding, their sandpaper-like skin causing nasty abrasions.

Dogfish are caught mainly by boat anglers, although bull huss are occasionally taken at night by rock anglers.

Tackle

Both types of spotted dogfish are bottom feeders. For this reason they are best fished for with a standard running leger rig. Neither fish is a shy feeder and a yard (metre) long trace is perfectly suitable. Bull huss have sharp teeth and so the trace should be made up from 40 lb (18.1 kg) breaking strain wire on 100 lb (45 kg) long-liners' nylon. Hooks of size 6–0 or 8–0 are ideal. Neither species of dogfish is a particularly strong fighter and a 20 or 30 lb (9.1 or 13.6 kg) class outfit will subdue even the largest bull huss.

On occasion large numbers of hefty bull huss may come from one particular area. Hardly a shoaling species, they normally congregate only to take advantage of a readily available food supply. In this sort of situation sport can be fast and furious. On one such occasion I was fishing at night for conger in a rugged area to the east of Mevagissey, in Cornwall. The water was about 100 ft (30 m) deep and the bottom excessively rough. We had stopped on the way to catch two boxes of mackerel and felt confident of a good night's sport. The mark we intended to fish was noted for conger in the 20–35 lb (9.1–15.9 kg) class. Occasionally it produced much bigger eels, and with luck this would be *the* night. Once anchored we cut up bait, attached leads and sent our baited hooks down into deep, dark water. The night was warm and overcast, with hardly a breath of wind to ripple the sea surface. A perfect night for conger, or so we thought.

For the first 30 minutes nothing much happened, but then the bites started: bouncing thumps that told their own story. Bull huss — not one or two but dozens. With six rods on board, much of the time four rods were in action simultaneously. The skipper worked flat out to clear lines and stow fish. Finally, at a little after midnight, bites slowed and then ceased. I never knew just how many big bull huss we had during that session. The skipper said he had stopped counting at fifty. Most of the fish weighed about 13 lb (5.9 kg), so the total weight for the night was extremely high. It was the best single bull huss session I have ever experienced. Obviously the fish had shoaled to take advantage of dense pout or pilchard shoals at exactly the same time and in the same place as we had anchored.

SPURDOG

Of similar size to the bull huss, the spurdog is by contrast very much a shoal fish. So large are the shoals that at times it is difficult to get away from them. A much harder-fighting species than the buss huss, the spurdog is popular with the majority of anglers. It is easy to catch because it is food mad. The quality of the bait is immaterial: fresh or stale fish or squid — it is all the same to the hungry spurdog. I suppose that, given such vast shoals, food is always at a premium and the fish work on a 'first come, first served' basis. Unlike all the other dogfish species, the spurdog will feed at all depths. Shoal members will start to follow hooked fish up towards the surface and at such times they can often be caught just below the boat keel.

The largest shoals of spurdog are normally found close to but out of a main flow of tide. Some of the largest catches I can recall have come from the west coast of Scotland or the north coast of Northern Ireland. I remember one huge catch made from Portrush on the Antrim coast. We were fishing close to the Balinjoy bank, hoping for a good catch of haddock or codling. We had fished the area two days previously and had done quite well. On this day we fished closer to the land. We should have known better. We started by using three baited feathers. Instantly we got typical spurdog bites that rattled the rod tips as the fish tore into the baits. Initially we were into three fish at a time. This soon became hard work and we changed to a simple one-hook paternoster. We were using fish-strip bait and there was not much sport to it: it was just drop down, wait for a bite to develop, strike and wind. Four hours of this and we had exhausted the fun. The fish hold was stuffed to overflowing with a multitude of squirming fish.

We moved off to a distant mark and spent the rest of the day catching big dabs for breakfast. Most spurdog are caught offshore in deepish water. On occasion, however, they come inshore to feed within casting range of beach anglers. A

SPURDOG

The spurdog is similar in appearance to the tope, and many novice anglers confuse the two. Spurdog, however, have a spike or spur at the leading edge of the dorsal fin. Although adult specimens grow to 3½–4 ft (1.1–1.2 m) in length, they do not reach the size of tope. This species is normally found in packs, and a pack of hungry spurdog will take any bait the angler cares to use. They do not confine their activities to the bottom alone, being content to feed at any level, provided they can obtain enough food.

The best way to catch spurdog is to leger a fish-fillet bait, although a string of baited mackerel feathers, or single or double-hook paternoster rigs, can also be used to good effect. Spurdog will strike at artificial baits, and I have had some big catches of these fish while using pirk baits for cod, coalfish and pollack. An artificial lure can be made more attractive by adding a sliver of fish or a squid strip. When handling spurdog, great care should be taken to avoid touching the claw-like spine on the dorsal fin.

---

favourite venue for shore fishermen is Chesil beach, in Dorset. Here the spurdog move inshore during November and December, this inshore movement normally coinciding with that of the sprat shoals. Again a simple one-hook paternoster rig baited with fish is the best technique. For shore fishing a 4–0 or 6–0 hook should be used. For boat fishing a 6–0 or 8–0 hook is better.

SMOOTH-HOUND

Although several species of smooth-hound exist, most anglers do not bother to differentiate between them. This is a mistake and has led to the loss of several records. The most common species has an overall grey skin, while the starry smooth-hound has a sprinkling of whitish spots over the otherwise grey background. Unlike the spurdog, the smooth-hound is a selective feeder, taking mostly worms and crustacea. The species is also much more localized in distribution, being found mainly over the Essex mud banks and the marshy sections of the Solent.

Large smooth-hound often feed in shallow water. This makes them popular with beach and dinghy fishermen. They also fall readily to baits presented on up-tide tackle. The best bait for both types of smooth-hound is crab: hard and soft-shelled shore crab or the easily obtainable hermit crab. Two or more large deshelled hermit crabs on a fine-wire 4–0 hook are the ideal bait. The most

popular fine-wire hook available is the chemically sharpened Kamasar round-bend Aberdeen-style pattern. For fishing deeper water with up-tide tackle a stronger hook is better. The O'Shaughnessy hook in the 2–0 size is the most popular pattern. A hooked smooth-hound fights very differently from a spur-dog. The former is a running fish which is capable of taking 50 or 60 yards (46–55 m) of line off the reel spool at high speed. Spurdog do not make long runs, preferring to circle round under the rod tip. In shallow water the smooth-hound may also leap clear of the water, which the spurdog never attempts.

Smooth-hound are very much a summer species. They are inshore from June until October, and after this period they either cease feeding or move offshore. When a smooth-hound picks up a juicy bait there is usually no warning. For this reason the reel should be left out of gear but with the ratchet in the 'on' position. For down-tide boat fishing in conventional style the rod should be held with the

Smooth-hound like this fish don't grow to a large size; but what they lack in weight they make up for in speed. These sharks can be taken off the shore or from boats, the favourite baits being worm or crab.

SMOOTH-HOUND

The smooth-hound fights harder than any other member of the dogfish family. Size for size, its fighting ability is similar to that of the tope. Indeed, the general appearance of the adult fish is very similar to that of a small tope. It does not, however, have the graceful shape of the tope, and its fins are rather large in comparison with its body.

Instead of having proper teeth, the smooth-hound has lips that are covered with hard slabs, similar to those of the skate and ray. Like most of the dogfish family, the smooth-hound is a confirmed bottom feeder but, unlike other dogfish, it rarely eats fish, preferring to feed on worms and crabs. Smooth-hound of up to 5 ft (1.5 m) long have been caught commercially, and I have seen specimens of over 20 lb (9.1 kg) caught on rod and line.

reel in the open position and the ratchet off. The ball of the thumb is used to brake the reel spool. In this way a taking fish can be allowed to run without feeling any drag. Once it has taken 15–20 yards (14–18 m) of line the spool can be locked up, leaving the fish to practically hook itself as it pulls the rod hard down.

Not an endangered species, the smooth-hound is nevertheless very localized in its distribution. To conserve fish stocks most thinking anglers now work on the catch-and-release principle. A great little fighting fish, the smooth-hound is well worth preserving. In this way stocks may increase or at worst maintain present levels, providing sport for future anglers.

5

Flatfish

FLOUNDER

Despite their small size flounder are still one of the most popular sea fish on the British list. In the past some anglers devoted their angling careers to the improvement of flounder-fishing techniques. The most notable of these anglers was the late John P. Garrard, who wrote under the name 'Seangler'. His book *Sea Angling with the Baited Spoon*, published in 1960, is still regarded as the best book on flounder and other flatfish.

Tackle

Even a big flounder is light compared with many sea species, and so most anglers use fresh-water tackle. For boat fishing an 8 ft (2.4 m) light carbon or fibreglass spinning rod is ideal. For shore work a 10 ft (3 m) carp rod or a 12 ft (3.6 m) light beach caster can be used. Heavy line is not needed, so a medium-sized fixed-spool reel is suitable for all styles of angling.

Methods

Flounder can be caught on static leger tackle, worm being the most productive bait. But probably the best and most interesting technique is to spin with a baited spoon. Originally this method was devised by J.P. Garrard for flounder fishing in Langstone harbour, Hampshire. Subsequently it was found to work wherever flounder congregate. The theory is that large flounder see what appears to be a small flounder dragging away a worm. The larger fish then sets about robbing the smaller fish and ends up on the hook.

Flounder spoons are now manufactured in a variety of colours, sizes, and materials. For use in shallow water a 2 or 2½ in (5 or 6 cm) white plastic spoon is perfect. Where there is a strong tidal flow a polished metal spoon should be

With the onset of winter, flatfish like this plump Irish flounder move inshore to feed. This one took a lugworm from Fenit pier.

substituted, the extra weight of the metal helping to hold the spoon and bait on the sea bed. In Cornwall the Fowey river experts use huge, home-made spoons hammered out of sheet copper. These extra-large spoons have accounted for some monster flounders. The flounder spoon rig (see Fig. 17)is simple, the only critical factor being the length of trail between spoon and hook. The maximum should be 1½–2 in (4–5 cm) – anything longer or shorter than this seldom produces fish.

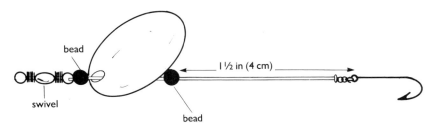

FIGURE 17   Use a white plastic or silver spoon between two beads. Bait the hook as this often proves deadly.

FLOUNDER

The flounder is a small, thick-bodied flatfish. Its head and mouth are large, and it has powerful jaws armed with sharp conical teeth. In colour it varies considerably from one locality to another. The back is usually greyish-brown, but I have seen many darker specimens. The underside is normally white. Occasional specimens have red spots on the back, like the plaice, and some have dark markings on both sides. The flounder can be caught at practically any time of year, although the winter is best. It is a real cold-weather fish, and will often feed when sea temperatures are so low that nothing else will stir itself to look at a bait.

Flounder have a wide distribution, being found all round Britain and Ireland. They show a marked preference for fresh or brackish water, often gathering in harbours, creeks and estuaries. They will also travel considerable distances upriver, and there are records of their having been caught far inland.

The average weight of rod-caught flounder is about ¾ lb (0.3 kg), but specimens of over 4 lb (1.8 kg) occur. Flounder are active fish which live mainly on crustacea, worms and small fish, but they also eat small shore crabs and sand shrimps.

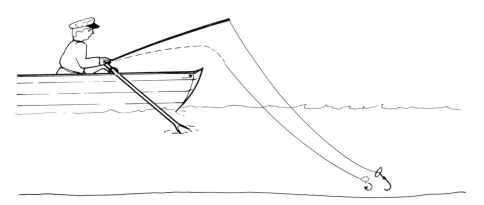

FIGURE 18   The dotted line shows how the rod tip drags over when a flounder takes the bait.

A baited spoon rig can be trolled behind a slowly rowed dinghy or it can be cast from an anchored boat. The best results are achieved when the bait is worked directly over the sea bed. Always fish the spoon with the tidal flow. I often see anglers fishing against the current and catching nothing for their efforts. Flounder normally swim and feed with the flow and a bait presented against the run of tide must appear totally unnatural. When a bite occurs it is essential to ignore the preliminary twitches and keep the spoon and bait moving. Never stop the forward motion of the lure or the flounder will take instant fright and vacate the area. Provided you keep the rig on the move, the flounder will nibble its way up the worm and virtually hook itself. On its day the baited spoon can be deadly. I remember one Boxing Day session on the Lymington river which produced 41 flounders to two rods. The river must have been paved with fish that day. We worked the margins of the boat channel and got a fish each cast.

PLAICE

Since they are prized as a table fish, plaice are a particularly sought after species. Like most fish they have their peak seasons. Early spring is when the big bags of plaice occur. Later in the year is the time for the odd very big fish. In recent seasons plaice fishing has become extremely popular. There are plaice hotspots such as Dartmouth, in Devon, and some Scottish sea lochs hold huge quantities of plaice. No doubt in time these will also become popular venues.

PLAICE

One of the best-known flatfish, the plaice has its eyes and its coloured half on its right side. Like most 'flatties', it varies in colour from one locality to another, but a typical specimen is brownish on the eye side and has white underparts. The back is heavily spotted with large orange or red blotches. Plaice to over 8 lb (3.6 kg) have been caught, but the average weight is 1 ½ lb–2 lb (0.7–0.9 kg). A fish of over 5 lb (2.3 kg) may be regarded as a really good catch.

They are widely distributed, being found around most of the British Isles, although they are commonest over offshore banks or skerries, or in areas where the sea bed is sand, mud or shell grit. Shellfish, particularly mussels, form the basic diet of the adult plaice, but marine worms, shrimps, soft crabs, small fish and starfish are also eaten.

Tackle

The choice of tackle depends on the area you intend to fish. In sheltered estuaries the tackle recommended for flounder (see page 57) will suffice. Where the fish lie in heavy tide stronger tackle is needed. Even then it pays to fish as light as possible. Several years ago I spent three days plaice fishing over the Dartmouth skerries. Here I drift-fished comfortably with an 11 ft (3.3 m) fibreglass pike rod and a small multiplier loaded with 12 lb (5.4 kg) breaking strain line. The best fish of the trip weighed 5 ¼ lb (2.4 kg).

Terminal tackle

When plaice are in a feeding mood they can be caught in twos and threes on a multiple-hook rig. The most popular tackle is a three-hook paternoster trot (see Fig. 19), of which there are many variations. Some incorporate plastic or wire booms (see Fig. 20). For normal conditions a single-hook running leger is more than adequate. At Dartmouth the leger rig is used for drift fishing, the trace being extended to 10 ft (3 m) or more (see Fig. 21). A leger rig can be greatly enhanced by adding half a dozen brightly coloured beads directly behind the hook (see Fig. 22). Red/white and red/yellow are the favourite combinations. I am told that fluorescent green beads are also great fish attractors. The rather old-fashioned

A fine 5¼ lb (2.4 kg) plaice caught by the author. This fish came from the skerries off Dartmouth, Devon. The bait was a cocktail of worm and hermit crab.

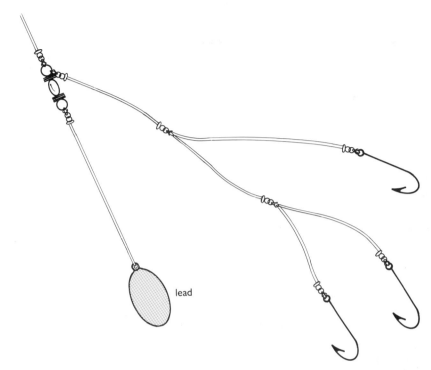

lead

FIGURE 19   A three-hook paternoster trot is the most popular tackle for plaice.

wander tackle (see Fig. 23) is still a good way to take plaice. This rig incorporates two spiral leads to hold the bait hard down. Spiral leads have a habit of coming off the line when used as bought. To avoid this the lead should be bent as shown (see Fig. 24).

At Dartmouth we used the long-trace running leger. This worked fine until the tide picked up speed. When this happened bites ceased altogether. It was obvious to me that the increased tidal flow was lifting the bait way up off the bottom. To counteract this tendency I pinched several swan shot onto the trace above the hook and beads. The shot took the bait back to fish level, and by adding or subtracting shot to suit the prevailing tides we were able to fish effectively throughout the day.

When fishing for plaice and other small flatfish a size 1 or 2 long-shanked narrow-gape flatfish hook should be used. Combination (cocktail) baits are often very killing. At Dartmouth we used worm and hermit crab tail to good effect. Worm and sand eel or squid strip can be equally deadly.

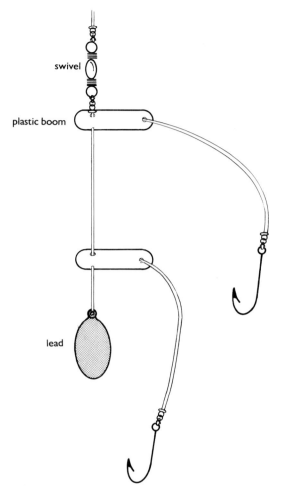

swivel

plastic boom

lead

FIGURE 20   A plastic-boom paternoster is often successful.

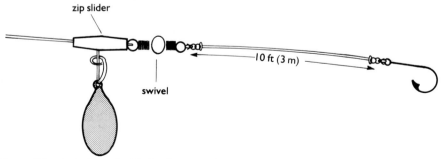

zip slider

swivel

10 ft (3 m)

FIGURE 21   A single or double-hook running leger is also useful. This is the Dartmouth plaice rig.

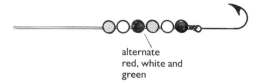

FIGURE 22   Coloured attractor beads work well. Vary the colours and pattern.

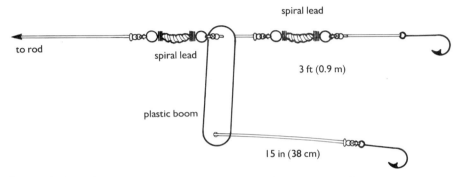

FIGURE 23   Wander tackle rolls slowly over the sea bed, searching out the bottom as it goes. It is the favourite terminal tackle of plaice specialists.

FIGURE 24   A spiral lead should be bent to stop it sliding up the line.

Other smaller flatfish

Dabs, sole, scaldfish, megrim and several other small flatfish can be taken on the type of tackle recommended for plaice (see page 61). Dabs prefer a strip of fish or squid, whereas sole prefer worm or peeler crab.

TURBOT AND BRILL

Both species are a prize catch for the boat angler. The turbot being the largest and most popular of the two species. Large turbot hold a subtle fascination for many anglers. Coverack, Dartmouth, and Weymouth are the main turbot ports, but the Varne Bank, off Dover, is another hotspot. Turbot have a wide distribution but are commonest in big tide areas such as the Antrim coast of Northern Ireland, where I have caught turbot of over 20 lb (9.1 kg).

TURBOT

It is difficult to confuse the turbot with other members of the flatfish family, with the possible exception of brill. The eyes and the coloured half are on the upper, left side of its body. Its back is normally greyish-brown, with a thick freckling of darker spots and blotches. Variable colouration is seen, depending to a large extent on what sort of sea bed the fish was feeding over when caught.

Turbot are usually caught during spring and summer, but in very deep water can be taken at almost any time of year. The species has a wide distribution. Big turbot like to live and feed in fast, heavy water, a prime example of which is the Shambles Bank, off Weymouth, once the most famous mark in Britain for big turbot.

Large baits are essential. This species is a true predator, with a big mouth and sharp teeth that are ideally suited to catch and hold any bait-sized fish that comes within reach. Turbot reach a weight of at least 35 lb (15.8 kg), but a rod-and-line angler who catches a 20 lb (9.1 kg) specimen should be proud.

Large turbot like to live and feed very near to offshore sand banks, where they take up station on the down-tide side of the bank (see Fig. 25).

FIGURE 25   Fish for down-tide turbot with the boat turned into the tide and up-tide from the bank.

Normally a solitary species, small colonies of brill often gather in food-rich areas. Once on a fishing trip to Alderney I was taken to fish an inshore bank that was reputed to hold both brill and blonde ray. The bait was live sand eel fished on up-tide tackle. On the first cast I caught a brill of 6 lb (2.7 kg). This was quickly followed by a further brace of brill and half a dozen blonde ray to 29 lb (13.2 kg). With only one live eel left I made my cast and within minutes had a 6 lb (2.7 kg) bass to round the season off.

BRILL

Smaller, although very similar in appearance, large brill are often mistaken for medium-sized turbot. The body of an adult brill is more oval than that of a turbot and the upper dorsal fin extends right down over its eyes (the upper dorsal fin of the turbot is shorter). Like the turbot, the brill varies considerably in colour from one area to another. Generally, the back is greyish-brown, with a heavy freckling of dark spots and whitish patches. The underside is white, although as in most 'flatties' (including turbot), partial colouring on the underside is fairly common.

Brill reach a maximum weight of around 15 lb (6.8 kg), although the average-sized fish weighs between about 5 and 8 lb (2.3–3.6 kg). Brill are probably far more plentiful in British waters than most anglers realize, and, like the turbot, are commonest off the south and south-west coast. Brill are active fish which live close to the sea bed, where they feed mainly on small fish and prawns. They are also fond of lugworm, and many of the big brill caught are taken unintentionally on rag or lugworm intended for plaice. If deadbait is used, it should be as fresh as possible, for brill are not scavengers and rarely take stale bait.

Tackle

In areas where the tide permits, up-tide tackle can provide first-class sport with turbot and brill. There are many up-tide rods on the market, most come in two unequal sections (a short butt and a long tip). This arrangement gives casting power. These rods are used in conjunction with a small multiplying reel of the Shimano Triton Speedmaster type. The reel line should have a breaking strain of 15 lb (6.8 kg). Thirty feet (9 m) of 30 lb (13.6 kg) nylon should be used as a shock leader. This is important, for a 'crack off' in a boat could be fatal. A heavy shock leader should cut the risk of such an accident to a minimum. For standard boat fishing a 30 or 50 lb (13.6 or 22.6 kg) class boat rod should be used. When

Brill are never big but are highly prized as table fish. Like the turbot, they normally fall to sand eel or fish strip baits.

choosing a rod of this kind make certain it has a roller tip ring. Wire line is often an essential part of turbot and brill fishing. To fish wire properly a roller tip is essential.

I use a Shimano TLD 15 reel with wire line and the larger TLD 20 with nylon. A big flatfish 'kiting' against a heavy tide quickly shows up any defect in a reel. My experience with the Shimano has shown that, like the old-fashioned star-drag Penn reels, they are built for heavy work. Turbot and brill are bottom feeders and are best caught on static or semi-static bait. To give the bait more appeal the trace should be 6–8 ft (1.8–2.4 m) in length. Hooks should be chosen first for their strength and then honed for maximum sharpness. Probably the best hook for big flatfish is a 6–0 or 8–0 O'Shaughnessy pattern. For up-tiding, much smaller hooks of the same pattern should be used, 2–0 or 4–0 being almost perfect. Turbot have sharp little teeth and so a heavy-duty nylon trace should be used, the ideal breaking strain of which is 60–80 lb (27.2–36.2 kg).

HALIBUT

Although halibut are true flatfish, they are the monsters of the family. One commercially caught specimen weighed 625 lb (283 kg) and had been gutted beforehand. The rod-caught record currently stands at 234 lb (106 kg). Larger fish have been hooked and lost. Commercial fishing has wiped out many halibut hotspots, and Orkney and Shetland are now the only places left in Britain where you can hope to contact one of these huge predatory 'flatties'.

Tackle

The few anglers who have caught halibut advocate 50 lb (22.6 kg) or even 80 lb (36.2 kg) class rods and 6–0 size reels to match. Line should have a breaking strain of 60–80 lb (27.2–36.2 kg). The reel should hold a minimum of 400 yards (366 m) of line. Hooks should be Mustad Seamaster shanked, size 10–0 or 12–0. The trace should be made of 100 lb (45 kg) long-liners' nylon. Only the best heavy-duty swivels should be used.

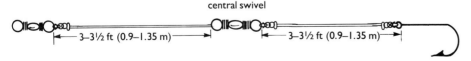

central swivel

|← 3–3½ ft (0.9–1.35 m) →| |← 3–3½ ft (0.9–1.35 m) →|

FIGURE 26   A central barrel swivel is used to join two lengths of 150–200 lb (60–80 kg) long-line nylon. Halibut traces need to be made from the best materials available.

HALIBUT

Halibut are large and strong enough to be regarded as a game-fishing species. Specimens of up to 300 lb (136 kg) have been caught fairly frequently by commercial methods. Every halibut taken on rod and line makes front-page news in the angling press, for such a catch remains a rare event, and few anglers can claim to have hooked, let alone landed, a halibut.

The halibut's body is more elongated and rounded than that of most other flatfish. The general colour is a greenish-brown, with white underparts. The mouth is large and the jaws are filled with sharp teeth. A northern species, the halibut is commonest in arctic or sub-arctic regions. It is a solitary creature which lives by catching small coalfish, cod, herring, skate, lobsters, and crabs – in fact, practically anything sizeable it can find.

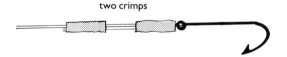

FIGURE 27 Crimps can be used to secure a hook or swivel to long-line nylon.

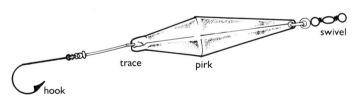

FIGURE 28 Halibut are predatory and a large pirk lure of this type is ideal for catching good fish. Cheap pirk-like lures can be made from lead-filled chrome tubing. Flatten the ends and drill, then fit a split pin.

Methods

The few rod-caught halibut have fallen to bottom-fished whole fish baits presented on running leger, or on huge pirk-style lures attached to a 12 in (30 cm) trace and a huge 12–0 hook baited with a whole fish or a fillet of fish (see Fig. 28).

6

Ling

Long, lean and powerful, the ling looks like a cross between a conger eel and a cod. Although not a particularly attractive fish, it is none the less popular with boat fishermen, especially wreck anglers. Essentially a deep-water species, ling are often encountered in huge numbers. In the 'early days' of wreck fishing during the 1960s, when virgin wrecks still existed, top skippers used to reckon it took three days' hard fishing to clear the ling off the top of a wreck. Once the ling packs had been wiped out it was possible to fish into the wreck for cod and big conger. At that time thousands of pounds of ling were caught in a single two- or three-hour session. I have seen days when over one hundred ling in the 15–25 lb (6.8–11.3 kg) range have been caught by six competent anglers. At first all the massive catches were made by wreck boats operating off Devon and Cornwall. In later years, however, it has been found that any English Channel wreck sunk in more than 35 fathoms (64 m) of water is capable of producing ling by the ton.

There is no trick to ling fishing. Basically an ever-hungry eating machine, a big ling is probably the easiest of fish to fool. I remember one wreck known as the Daddy Longlegs. Situated close to the mid-Channel buoy, the 'Daddy' is 35 miles (56 km) off the Dorset coast. I was fortunate enough to be on the first expedition to fish this wreck. We left Mudeford harbour at 4.30 am aboard Anton Proctor's boat *Avon Valleys*. Anton was an old friend from my commercial fishing days. How he found the Decca number for the 'Daddy', I have no idea; nor did I care much. The excitement of a crack at a new wreck brings on a surge of adrenalin that drives everything from an angler's mind except the fishing. Halfway to the wreck we stopped to feather string after string of plump mackerel. I remember that I foulhooked a fat pilchard, the first of its kind I had ever seen off Dorset. With ample bait aboard we finally reached the wreck itself.

Every wreck angler has his favourite terminal rig. I chose to fish a large red and silver pirk bait. To avoid foulhooking fish I had removed the giant factory-fitted treble hook and substituted 10 in (25 cm) of 150 lb (68 kg) long-liners' nylon. This was knotted and crimped (see Fig. 27). Knots in heavy nylon can spring out

Ling of this size (30 lb – 13.6 kg) normally live on wrecks. This superb fish was caught in 45 fathoms of water on a whole mackerel.

under pressure. The crimp stops this occurring and makes a nice neat finish to a heavy-duty trace. The hook was a well-honed O'Shaughnessy size 10–0. Once it was knotted to the 60 lb (27.2 kg) reel line and baited with half a mackerel, I had a rig which would take ling, cod and even conger.

As Anton set up the drift we stood in a line down the gunnel, reels out of gear, thumbs braking the spool. At the words 'Go for it', six thumbs lifted and six assorted sets of end tackle vanished into more than 40 fathoms (73 m) of dark blue water. The trick to wreck fishing is to know when the tackle bumps the wreck. The second this occurs line must be retrieved to bring the bait up above the wreckage. Ten turns of the reel is normally sufficient and on this occasion I had just stopped cranking the handle when I felt a slow dragging on the rod tip. Big as ling are, they seldom slam into a bait. The moment I felt the dragging I started to turn the reel handle. Striking in that depth of water is pointless. The elasticity of the nylon acts as a buffer. Wind in slowly instead and you can feel the fish onto the hook. Once this happens it pays to pump and wind down to the fish as fast as possible. A big, flustered ling is very capable of power-diving back into the security of the wreckage. Like most ling this fish fought for a minute or two before the pressure change hit it, allowing me to get it up to the surface where it was quickly gaffed, unhooked and dropped into the fish hold.

LING

Ling are members of the cod family. They have long bodies, broad heads and wide, tooth-filled mouths, two dorsal fins and a single long barbule under the chin. Ling vary in colour from one area to the next, but are usually grey or greenish-brown. In some ling, particularly smaller fish, the body is mottled with darker spots and blotches. Like conger, ling can grow to vast size, and specimens of over 100 lb (45 kg) have been taken by commercial fishing. Yet any angler fortunate enough to boat a ling of over 25 lb (11.3 kg) can be proud, although fish of over 50 lb (22.6 kg) have been taken on rod and line.

As a fighting species, ling are a better proposition than conger. Like conger, they love wrecks and sunken rocks; but unlike them, often feed well up off the bottom. Large ling can occasionally be encountered over flat ground. At one time ling stocks were thought to be confined to West Country, Irish and Scottish marks, but evidence now shows that they are probably distributed right round Britain and Ireland.

Ling are greedy fish. Unlike the conger, which tends to be a cautious feeder, a big ling is a voracious biter which pulls the rod tip down hard as it engulfs the bait. Ling are predators and can be caught on all types of squid and fish bait. On wrecks, fresh mackerel are the most successful lure. Ling fall easily to baited pirk lures. The bigger the bait the better it seems to work.

With a fresh bait on I dropped back and instantly hooked up on a second fish. The other anglers were having similar success and the first drift put nine hefty ling in the boat. With an average weight of over 15 lb (6.8 kg) the catch totalled well over 100 lb (45 kg) of fish on the first drift. But with the best of the tide still to come we knew we were in for a bonanza. On this occasion one of the party fished a baited pirk and three baited 'Muppets' (plastic squid). The inevitable happened: he hit three or possibly four big fish at one time. No tackle can take this sort of strain, and he lost the lot. The moral is simple: don't be greedy. Fish a one-hook rig and you will rarely get smashed up.

As the day continued the fish began to change. First came wave after wave of ling, so fast that both skipper and crewman worked flat out to gaff and unhook them. Ling have a formidable array of large, sharp teeth. To save time and fingers each fish was unhooked with a 'T' bar (see Fig. 14). This home-made disgorger, very strong and efficient, is simply hooked over the bend of the big hook and then, with a quick shake, even the deepest set hook is jolted free. It is equally good for any big fish. With an estimated 2,000 lb (907 kg) of ling in the boat we suddenly started to catch cod and big ones at that. Later, back at Mudeford, the best cod of the day weighed in at 44 lb (20 kg). Intensive cod and ling bashing can be an exhausting pastime. In an attempt to gain some respite a couple of the party changed to Red Gill sand eels. Instantly they found the pollack, fat, fit fish of 12–15 lb (5.4–6.8 kg), each arriving at the surface like a bar of living gold. What a day! An estimated 4,000 lb (1,814 kg) of prime fish, every one hauled up from 40 fathoms (73 m) or more. It was a typical ling wreck trip but with a wedge of bonus fish to add interest.

Not all ling are found over wrecks. In all areas the bigger ling are very much a deep-water species. At present most of the known and fished wrecks have been sunk in 35–50 fathoms (64–91 m). It could well be that the really large ling, fish in the record-breaking class, are found in much deeper water. In Northern Ireland I fished off Rathlin Island to take ling out of 120 fathoms (219 m) of water. Small specimens can also be taken over reefs. Hat Rock off Fowey, in Cornwall, is often thick with small ling, providing holiday anglers with good sport. The normal technique is to fish a single-hook paternoster rig baited with fish strip. Much further north, off Orkney, local specialists use a wire boom and a spoon blade (see Fig. 29) to attract and catch ling. In Orcadian waters ling are important make-weight fish in local competitions, in which this spoon and bait combination proves deadly.

It would seem that modern day ling are much smaller than the fish of the last century. Old records reveal that ling of over 100 lb (45 kg) were regarded as common. The present rod-caught record ling weighed 53 lb (24 kg), a small fish compared with those of yesteryear. Ling are also now being caught in shallow water, particularly off the Isle of Wight, where increasing numbers of big fish are caught in water of about 20 fathoms (37 m). All these inshore ling catches are made during the winter months. Possibly these fish grew big because of the increase in sprat stocks. Whatever the reason, they make a welcome addition to the winter cod.

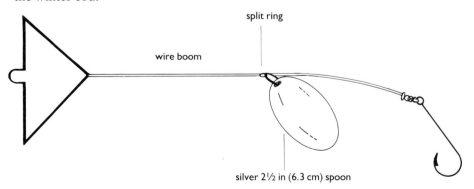

FIGURE 29 Orkney-style ling tackle. This looks unconventional but works successfully.

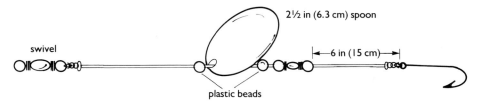

FIGURE 30   A simple attractor spoon, used in front of natural bait to add flash. The spoon is held in place by two plastic beads.

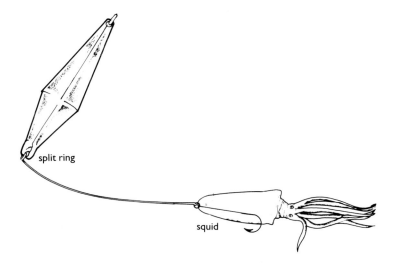

FIGURE 31   A pirk with an 8-inch (20 cm) wire trace between its split ring and the hook, which is baited with squid or mackerel. This is lethal for good-sized cod or ling.

TACKLE

Ling are best caught on conger or cod-weight gear. For deep-water work a 50 lb (22.6 kg) class outfit is perfect, while for inshore fishing a 30 lb (13.6 kg) class rig is recommended. Remember that ling have a mouthful of large, sharp, cutting teeth, which can easily cut through 60 lb (27.2 kg) nylon. To avoid 'cut offs' it is essential to use either a heavy wire trace or, better still, a length of 150 lb (68 kg) long-liners' nylon, which is extra tough and yet more supple than wire. After each fish it pays to run the trace through your fingers. At the slightest sign of wear it should be instantly replaced.

7

Mackerel and Garfish

Probably the easiest of all sea fish to catch, the mackerel is an ideal quarry for the light-tackle enthusiast or the fresh-water angler on a seaside holiday. To get the best out of these sporting fish it is advisable to catch them singly. If you want to fill your freezer or bait box then use a set of size 4 or 6 feathers. Originally feathers were simply dyed chicken hackle feathers lashed to the shank of a tinned hook. Nowadays they are mostly made from various man-made fibres (see Fig. 32). Mackerel are attracted to movement rather than colour and a set of feathers that can be made to move in a fish-like manner will soon attract and catch mackerel in quantity. Boat anglers simply jig the feathers up and down by raising and lowering the rod tip.

Although generally regarded as a boat-fishing technique, feathering can also be used from the beach or rocks. At West Bay on Dorset's Chesil beach, anglers use a beach rod to cast a set of four feathers out as far as possible, retrieving them at high speed. To give the feathers extra movement the rod tip is swung from side to side. When the mackerel are inshore in large numbers, huge catches are made. However, catching four fish at once is not a sporting style of angling. It is better to use a longer, lighter rod to cast a smaller lead and a single feather. With this sort of rig each mackerel is given a chance to show its fighting ability to the full.

On a recent trip to Chesil I took along an 11 ft (3.3 m) carbon carp rod, a Shimano BioMaster reel designed for distance casting and a selection of single feathers. For long-range casting some of the modern plastic or Mylar feathers are more useful than the traditional patterns constructed from natural feathers. Traditional feathers are bulky and reduce casting distances considerably. They are also less durable than feathers constructed from man-made fibre. On the day I fished the sea was calm and the conditions near perfect. With a 2 oz (55 g) lead and 10 lb (4.5 kg) line I was able to drop the feather about 130 yards (120 m) offshore. Often bites would come on the drop. At this range each fish fought a hard, fast battle for freedom. As the tide continued to rise the fish moved inshore. At this stage I switched tackle, discarding the feather and lead in favour

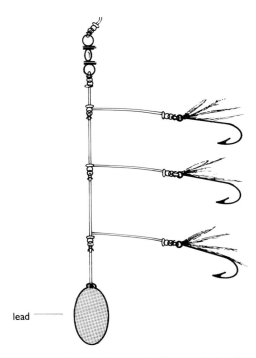

lead

FIGURE 32 Mackerel feathers are deadly. Set your feathers at the level at which mackerel are feeding and then raise and lower the rod tip. A series of knocks will indicate that mackerel are hanging themselves on the hooks.

of an extra-heavy Abu Toby lure. This long, thin but heavy spoon proved deadly. Moreover, it put me in direct contact with the fish, adding a new dimension to the sport. Keeping only a dozen or so fish for food, I returned the others unharmed. Excessive commercial netting has had a detrimental effect on mackerel stocks, but anglers can help to safeguard future stocks by sticking to self-imposed bag limits.

FLOAT FISHING

Apart from spinning and feathering, float tackle can be used to catch mackerel and garfish. Some of my earliest memories of sea fishing are of catching both species from Mevagissey Quay. In those days sea floats were huge. Luckily, fish were more numerous and less finicky than they are today and the size of float did not stop them biting. Nowadays I still like to float-fish for mackerel and the

---

MACKEREL

Mackerel are predators, feeding on the fry of herring, sprat and pilchard, and on sand eels. During the spring mackerel feed on the great banks of drifting plankton, but at all other times are fish eaters. Mackerel grow to well over 4 lb (1.8 kg), but most rod-caught specimens weigh 1–2 lb (0.45–0.9 kg).

Weight-for-weight, mackerel are without doubt the gamest fish any angler could wish to catch. Anything shiny, which spins, wobbles or vibrates as it is being retrieved will bring an instant response if mackerel are on the move. My favourite spinners for this sort of work are bar spoons such as the Voblex or medium Mepps.

Mackerel are much easier to hook than garfish for, although both species hit a bait as hard as they can, the narrow, hard beak of the garfish does not give much purchase to the hook point. The big mouth of the mackerel, by contrast, gives a secure hold every time, and so few mackerel are lost in comparison with garfish. Both species seem to be attracted to fast-moving baits. Therefore it is best to retrieve at speed, and forget about working the bait up and down or from side to side to simulate the movement of a wounded or sick fish.

---

acrobatic garfish. The techniques are the same, but the tackle is more refined: slim little sliding pike floats, a long, light rod and a modern fixed-spool reel in place of the old wooden centrepin of my childhood. The bait is the same: a long sliver cut from the side of a mackerel or garfish (see Fig. 33). The float is set to a depth of 2–4 yards (1.8–3.7 m). A tiny section of rubber band hitched to the line acts as a stop. The weight is a string of non-toxic split shot. Hooks are size 6 or 8 on the freshwater scale. Mackerel can be caught on larger hooks but garfish, with their bird-like beaks, need the smaller patterns. Bites are usually hard-hitting, taking the float straight down. Occasionally garfish will play with the bait but mostly they take it decisively. If a bite is missed on the strike leave the baited tackle where it is. Both mackerel and garfish will normally come back and take it again. Sometimes both species will feed just under the surface. This mainly occurs on hot, windless days when the sea is flat calm. Under such conditions garfish put up a magnificent battle, leaping repeatedly in their attempts to shake the hook. Diminutive though these fish may be, their fighting spirit is second to none. Garfish are edible but their bones are green. If you have no use for them, return them unharmed to the sea.

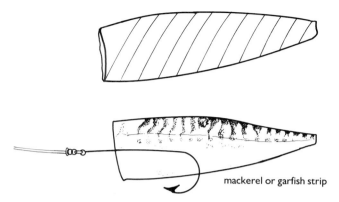

mackerel or garfish strip

FIGURE 33   Mackerel fillet makes a top bait. Cut the fillet from the side of your bait.

GARFISH

A hard-fighting fish to be found in company with mackerel shoals is the garfish. Many anglers seeing a garfish for the first time assume that it is some form of small swordfish, as its elongated body and bird-like beak give it the appearance of belonging to that family. If garfish grew to a respectable size, they would probably be the most sought-after species on the British list.

A hooked garfish puts on a spectacular display of acrobatics, spending as much of its time out of the water as in it. One of its favourite tricks is to stand on its tail and skitter across the surface for several yards before cartwheeling back into the sea. On light tackle any garfish, regardless of size, can be relied upon to put up a magnificent struggle before it is subdued.

Like mackerel, garfish have a wide distribution but are probably commonest along the southern and south-western coasts of the British Isles. They are essentially surface feeders, but during extremely bad weather they will hunt for food on the sea bed.

When I was skippering shark boats I used to take an ultra-light outfit to sea with me: a tiny spinning rod, a fixed-spool reel with 3 lb (1.4 kg) line, some small hooks and a few split shot. This outfit was brought into use when the shark lines were out and the rubby-dubby bag was spilling a trail of oil and fish offal.

Primarily intended as shark attractant, the 'dubby' soon brought in thousands of mackerel and garfish. A strip of fish on the hook, a single shot pinched on the line to weight it down, and the outfit was ready for action. The bait was simply dropped into the tide flow and allowed to drift away. Once it was away from the boat, the reel pick-up was engaged. Bites were detected by a finger on the line. On one occasion I caught and released more than 50 garfish and uncounted mackerel. On another a large porbeagle shark snapped up the mackerel strip seconds after it hit the water. I saw the fish take it but never felt the bite. The nylon parted instantly. This same outfit and technique can be used for pier and jetty fishing. Take along a little minced fish as groundbait.

8

Monkfish and Angler Fish

Neither the monkfish nor the angler fish is likely to win a beauty prize, for both are particularly ugly. But they do offer the boat angler the opportunity to catch a really big fish. Of the two species the monkfish is the more common but, with one exception, there are no set places to find them. Generally, they are nomadic, solitary wanderers that occur over a mud, sand or shingle bottom. The exception is the famous 'monk' hole off the town of Fenit, on Tralee Bay, in Co. Kerry. This hole is in fact a shallow depression in the mud. For some reason large numbers of big monkfish gather in this depression, making it easy for a visiting angler to catch a really large specimen. This mark is so small that local boatmen guard it jealously. Naturally, its contents are a valuable asset to both boatmen and the local hotels, and for this reason each hooked monkfish is returned alive and in good condition.

MONKFISH

Monkfish are the link between the shark and the skate. They are usually greyish-brown, and are often confused with the angler fish. The average weight of rod-caught monkfish is around 25–45 lb (11.3–20.4 kg), but specimens of up to 60 lb (27.2 kg) are by no means rare. Monkfish have a wide distribution, but are commonest in the southern half of the English Channel. Large monkfish are commonly caught off the south-west coast of Ireland. They are ungainly creatures incapable of showing any great turn of speed.

Monkfish fan the sea bed vigorously with their fins and then eat the small fish that are attracted by the cloudy water. Practically anything that swims and is small enough will be eaten by hungry monkfish, but small flatfish seem to be the main part of the diet. Monkfish are great scavengers and will eat any dead fish they find, irrespective of whether it is stale or fresh.

I have fished the hole only once, on a day when strong winds made it impossible to get out into deep water. We made up standard leger tackle using a short wire hook trace, baited an 8–0 hook with a mackerel fillet, and dropped it over the stern of the boat. I doubt if there was more than 6 ft (1.8 m) of water in the hole but it was full of fish. Twenty minutes and three 45 lb (20.4 kg) monkfish later I had had enough. The fish did not fight – they simply wallowed up to the boat, where the hook was levered out and they were set free to go back and wait for the next boatload of anglers. The largest monkfish I ever saw was caught from a 20 ft (6 m) mud hole to the east of Sowley submarine boom in the Solent. It took fish bait and apparently fought extremely well. Back at Lymington it weighed in at 64 lb (29 kg), a magnificent specimen of its kind.

The name monkfish is thought to derive from the fact that the fish resembles a monk's cowl. It is a primeval-looking creature with a foul temper. Even a small monkfish has a huge gash of a mouth filled with sharp cutting teeth. In a boat the monkfish has a nasty habit of snapping wildly at anything that comes within range, including unwary hands and feet. Great care must be taken when unhooking these fish. Normally a hooked 'monk' is brought to the side of the boat and the hook is cut free while the fish is still in the water. If it is required as a trophy it should be killed as quickly as possible. There is, however, little point in destroying a monkfish otherwise. The flesh is virtually inedible and the fish smells strongly of ammonia.

ANGLER FISH

Probably the ugliest species on the British list, the angler fish has a huge head and a tapering tail which make it easy to identify. Like the monkfish, it is a spring and summer visitor to British waters, spending the winter in deep water offshore.

Angler fish have a wide distribution and have been recorded in all parts of the British Isles. Confirmed bottom feeders, they live almost entirely on fish. Owing to their grotesque shape, they have to ambush their food, for they are incapable of fast bursts of speed and so are unable to pursue and catch prey. Although the angler fish cannot be classed as a true fighting fish, its bulk makes it a formidable opponent.

Very occasionally, angler fish will rise to the surface and try to engulf a sleeping sea bird. Like cod, they swallow all sorts of trash from the sea bed; jam jars, tins, sea weights, lumps of scrap metal, corks and bits of wood have all been found in their stomachs.

Monkfish are by no means common. Most are caught off the south coast of England or the west coast of Ireland. This 29-pounder (13.2 kg) was taken off the Isle of Wight. The bait was mackerel strip.

Oddly enough, the tail of the angler fish is delicious and is normally sold as monkfish. The only reason for this name change can be the even uglier appearance of the angler fish. Aptly named the fishing frog, the angler fish actually fishes for its food, using a 'rod' which sprouts from the top of its head. The end of this rod culminates in a leather-like flap which the fish waves about as a bait. Small fish come to investigate and are instantly engulfed by the angler. Few angler fish are ever caught intentionally, most being taken on baits intended for skate, tope or turbot.

Never a fussy feeder, the angler takes its food where it can find it. Several very large specimens have fallen to baited pirk-style lures fished on the edge of sunken wrecks. Very occasionally, particularly after stormy weather, angler fish come close inshore. Again, such fish are normally taken on baits intended for other species.

Under normal circumstances both monkfish and angler fish are caught on a standard running leger baited with whole live or dead fish or squid.

9

Mullet

One of the nice things about mullet fishing is that it is essentially a light-tackle sport. Not that mullet are small, for some grow to 12 lb (5.4 kg) or even 15 lb (6.8 kg). Irrespective of size, however, mullet are cautious, shy-biting fish quickly panicked by heavy tackle. Mullet fishing falls into three categories: harbour, rock, and estuary. Each habitat calls for a different approach, although mullet may move between harbours and rocky areas.

Where I live, near the Hampshire–Dorset border, the thin-lipped variety is the most prolific mullet. It seldom grows as large as the thick-lipped mullet, but it is still a very interesting fish to catch. Unlike the thick-lipped and golden grey mullet, the thin-lipped mullet will chase and take a baited spinner.

SPINNING

For me spinning for mullet is an established local technique, but it is rarely used elsewhere in Britain. I recall a session with northern angling writer Phil Williams. Phil has a collector's mania for fish species, and like a bird watcher he will travel anywhere in the hope of adding a new fish to his list of personally caught specimens. On this occasion thin-lipped mullet were his priority. Phil is always thorough, leaving little to chance. His plan was to trail his boat down to Hampshire, where we would try the local estuaries for mullet.

As the sun rose on our first day, we launched into the river and headed downstream to the local hotspot. As usual we both had brought far too much tackle and a battery of made-up rods bristled over the transom. At a point where the estuary narrowed, Phil swung his boat into position and I dropped the anchor. As the tide took up the slack we reached for our rods. Spinning for thin-lipped mullet is not difficult. But the choice of spoon is critical. In this case we were both using tiny, gold-coloured bar spoons with an orange-painted lead body. A touch of orange seems to drive these estuary mullet crazy. The spoon is not effective until the hook is tipped with a tiny 1 in (2.5 cm) section of ragworm (see Fig. 34). Having fished the area many times for mullet I had brought an ample supply of spinners and enough worms for a fish-packed day. As it turned out, I had done the right thing. Phil was first to hook up and as I waited with the landing net I could see mullet breaking surface all round the boat. This first fish was Phil's first-ever thin-lipped mullet and I could see he was pleased with it.

While Phil sorted out his fish and tackle I picked up my ultra-light spinning rod and flipped the baited spoon out 30 yards (27 m). Mullet seem to take a fast-moving spinner well and I cranked the reel handle rapidly to set the spoon blade churning through the water. Five yards (4.5 cm) from the boat a fish slammed solidly into the line, hooking itself firmly. Mullet are great fighters and despite its average size the thin-lipped is no exception. With the light rod and 4 lb (1.8 kg) breaking strain line I had no ability to bully the fish. Finally, however, the game little 2¼-pounder (1 kg) began to slow down. At this stage I was able to increase the pressure and force it into the waiting net. Two nice fish in the first two casts and more to come. We had decided on a bag limit of ten fish, which we reached within the first 30 minutes. After this we switched to a catch-and-release policy.

MULLET

There are three types of grey mullet in British waters: the thin-lipped, the thick-lipped and the least common, the golden grey, identifiable by its golden cheek patches. The small red mullet is rare. On average mullet weigh 1½–3 lb (0.7–1.4 kg). Any fish above 5 lb (2.3 kg) is a good catch, and anything over 6 lb (2.7 kg) is a specimen.

Mullet are shoal fish, the largest shoals comprising the smaller fish. The big fish are found only in small groups, and it is therefore very difficult to catch more than one or two large mullet in a session. With medium-sized fish, though, catches of up to a dozen are common. Mullet are a southern species. They are common from the Essex coast round to Land's End, and also round the Channel Islands and the south-west coast of Ireland. Many marks in Cornwall and Wales produce good catches of prime mullet. Huge specimens, to over 14 lb (6.3 kg), have been taken near the warm water outlets of power stations, and there is little doubt that constantly high sea temperatures promote rapid growth in mullet.

In the natural state, mullet feed mainly on algae and soft mud, from which they extract minute aquatic organism. Those which regularly feed on weed usually make poor table fish, as their flesh tastes strongly of weed and mud.

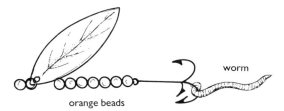

FIGURE 34   A mullet spoon baited with worm section. Use orange beads behind the spoon to add colour.

I cannot remember exactly how many fish we had before a turning tide carried the mullet shoal away, but something over 40 would be a good estimate. This number of thin-lipped greys on a single tide is a phenomenal bag – proof that on its day the baited spinner can be a deadly lure. If this technique works in one set of estuaries, as we proved, it should be just as deadly elsewhere. The trick, however, is to use only a bar spoon which has a bright orange body. Many companies produce this style of spinner, the best examples originating in France and Italy. Thin-lipped mullet are the only variety interested in spinners. Thick-lipped mullet are more of a browsing species.

FLOAT FISHING

When I fished the Fowey river at Golant, in Cornwall, the trick was to anchor a piece of bread crust on a long length of string (see Fig. 35). As the tide began to rise, huge shoals of mullet would work upriver over the barely covered mud flats. Sooner or later a fish would locate the anchored crust and start to pull at it. Within minutes other fish would appear and begin to mouth at the floating offering. The bread would begin to break up, loose particles drifting off on the tide. At this stage I would start to fish. The technique was to float fish using a bird-quill float with lead wire wound round its base. The bread was allowed to sink slowly and naturally, and the self-cocking float gave instant bite indication. The mullet fell for it every time. Obviously they saw my bread flake as a totally natural food item. Bites were bold and most mullet were hooked well inside the mouth. I have fished at Golant for many summers and never had a bad day's mullet fishing.

In mainland Britain mullet are essentially a summer species, June to mid September being the best time. With the onset of cold weather the shoals vanish, and that is the end of mullet fishing for another year unless the angler knows the secret of Alderney. From November to March this lovely member of the

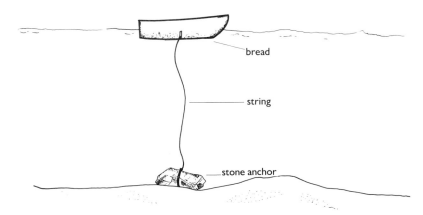

FIGURE 35   The anchored-crust method of groundbaiting is best when you are fishing in shallowish water. Mullet are quick to discover ground bait. A mixture of bran, chopped fish and pilchard oil provides a lethal mixture for prebaiting a gulley.

Channel Islands becomes a mullet angler's paradise. Shoals of big mullet, a thousand or more strong, invade Braye harbour while elsewhere smaller shoals crowd in to feed in a multitude of deep rock gullies. Over the seasons Alderney has produced many mullet of over 10 lb (4.5 kg). Even the average size ranges from 3 to 5 lb (1.4–2.3 kg) – heavy enough to attract mullet experts from all over Britain. Most local specialists and all visiting anglers use fresh-water tackle for Alderney mullet. A 12 or 13 ft (3.6 or 3.9 m) carbon float rod matched with a small lever-drag fixed-spool reel is standard equipment. A few anglers, like myself, use a centrepin trotting reel for most rock work. From the heights of Braye breakwater, however, a fixed-spool is more useful.

Over the years I have tried a variety of fixed-spools and have finally found one which I feel is perfect for mullet work. This is the Shimano GTM 2500, which has a particularly high rate of retrieve of 6:21. This rapid retrieve allows me to instantly regain contact with a hooked mullet that turns and runs towards me. The beauty of this sort of reel lies in its stern drag system and ultra-smooth clutch. Mullet are often lightly hooked and a clutch that has a tendency to 'snatch' can easily jerk a hook free. In the bad old days anglers used to backwind running fish. Modern clutch mechanisms allow a hooked mullet to fight against the clutch while minimizing the risk of the fish being lost.

Normally I fish for mullet with Alderney experts Roddy Hayes and Rob Labalistair, who know every inch of the island. They have evolved a 'shirvy' (groundbait) formula that cannot be bettered. It looks like an obnoxious mess, but this mixture of bran, meat, fish and blood really appeals to the mullet shoals.

A grand catch of Channel Island grey mullet. Taken off Alderney, all these fish were caught on freshwater float tackle baited with scraps of pork meat.

The secret of shirvy is do not overdo it. Roddy uses a large cook's spoon to flick out a tiny wedge of shirvy on the principle of little and not very often. On my first Alderney mullet hunt he informed me that too much groundbait and the mullet gorge themselves and refuse to take the hook bait. The aim is to stimulate their appetite but not feed them. Certainly, tiny dabs of shirvy flicked out into the tide flow soon attract mullet, and as soon as fish are seen in the area fishing can begin.

Using a Drennan loafer-style float can be a deadly technique. The float should be used bottom-end only and held in place with two locking shot (see Fig. 36). Fixed this way, it is ultra-sensitive, and the tiniest touch on the bait is sufficient to drag it down. The other non-toxic shot can be strung down the line bead-style or bunched directly under the float to allow the bait to free-fall through the water. Good as the float is as a bite detector, it must never be forgotten that its prime purpose is to support the bait at whatever depth the fish are feeding at. In clear conditions Alderney mullet anglers prefer to watch the bait rather than the float. Bait watching calls for intense co-ordination between eye and hand. When the bait vanishes, the strike must follow instantly.

On one of my visits to Alderney the mullet were concentrated off the very tip of the breakwater. On this occasion I was fishing with Rob Labalistair. The instant the shirvy hit the water, the fish moved in to mop up the tiny bait fragments. We were fishing small morsels of pork sliced from a fresh chop. Initially we fished in the normal way, with the split shot strung down the line beneath the float. But after a few casts it became clear that something was unnerving the packed and obviously hungry mullet. Time and again individual fish would move in to intercept a bait, but each time they would shy away at the very last second. To my mind, the spread shot was taking the bait down too fast. To overcome this we pushed the shot up to the float stem and began to fish 'on the drop'. This brought instant success. I missed a good fish and a second later Rob hit one of similar size. Like all Alderney mullet this one made a dash out into the main tide flow and used the force of the water to break for freedom. A less experienced angler might well have been 'smashed up', but Rob made no mistakes. Using the rod to apply sideways pressure, he soon had the fish worn down and out of the main current. Mullet fight to the end and this one was no exception. Finally, however, Rob was able to steer it over the big drop net.

With fish number one out of the water we were keen to get more. The first one weighed a little over 4½ lb (2 kg), but some of the shoal were larger. Another splatter of shirvy and in went our baits. I clearly saw the fish suck in the bait, and struck accordingly. The first rush of a big mullet on light tackle takes some stopping. This fish, like Rob's, swept out into the current, tearing line off the stern drag reel. Any attempt at stopping the fish would have resulted in an instant 'break off'. No matter how far and fast a hooked fish travels, it eventually begins to slow up. As mine burned itself out I was able to ease it out of

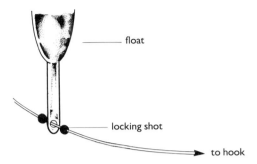

float

locking shot

to hook

FIGURE 36   Secure your float with locking shot. Mullet tackle is very light by sea-fishing standards and many anglers find it quite hard to adjust to it. Stick with it – float fishing is the best all-round method.

the main tide into a semi-slack area. There it continued to fight, using its broad tail to bore down deep. But steady rod pressure paid off and it rolled slowly into the big net. Almost identical in size to Rob's fish, it was a catch I was delighted to make.

In the next hour we took five more fish, all 'on the drop'. The best fish of the session weighed over 5 lb (2.3 kg). By normal standards for mullet fishing this was a red-letter day. Yet Alderney is a mullet haven capable of producing quality fish at almost anytime. At the tail end of 1988 I was there with Shimano tackle boss John Loftus. John is an old hand at mullet fishing on the Welsh coast, but had never sampled what Alderney has to offer. Unusually, the weather was vile. On the first day it was impossible to fish on the breakwater and we tried several rock marks. Unfortunately, the mullet failed to appear and it looked as though our trip would be a total washout. That night, however, the wind changed direction and by morning the sea had calmed enough for us to be able to fish the breakwater in safety. With a bucketful of shirvy and a box of white carp worms, we felt optimistic. We had arranged to fish with local angler Roddy Hayes and as we set out for the long walk to the end of the harbour arm I could sense his confidence.

On arrival at the fishing position we set up the tackle and began to introduce shirvy. For a while, nothing. Then suddenly the fish appeared: grey ghosts moving stealthily through the baited area. At times like this it is easy to make a mistake and put in too much groundbait. This can be disastrous, for mullet have only a small capacity for food. Too much shirvy and they fill up and vanish. Aware of this, we used the shirvy sparingly. Even so, we could see individual fish sucking in bait particles. One extremely bold fish even rose to intercept bait fragments that floated on the surface. Because the fish were tightly packed I decided not to fish but to act as netsman. But for over half an hour the fish ignored the worm baits. Then, suddenly, the situation changed and John's float vanished at high speed. It was a confident take and an easy fish to hook. From the start it was clearly a good fish and, like all large mullet, it used its tail and the tide flow to good effect. For over five minutes it gave as good as it got. In such conditions a match rod and 4 lb (1.8 kg) line have to be used carefully. Finally, its strength drained, the fish began to give ground. At this stage we were all anxious to see it and gain some idea of its size. When it did show it was obvious that it weighed over 5 lb (2.3 kg). Not a fish to be trifled with. Fortunately, it was so tired that it was soon in the drop net and on its way up the wall. Close to, it looked even bigger than our unanimous estimate of over 6 lb (2.7 kg), and on the scales it registered 6 lb 10 oz (3 kg). It was the third largest mullet of the Alderney season.

Naturally, John's magnificent fish fired our enthusiasm. Large mullet normally swim in small shoals, and with luck we would make contact with similar or possibly even larger specimens. Sad to say, it was not to be. Two more mullet were caught, both around 2½ lb (1.1 kg). When John's big fish made its first long seaward run, the rest of the shoal had obviously followed it out. This often happens and almost always the following fish take flight and vanish for good. Mullet are at best a cautious species, but they are plentiful in the southern half of Britain. The trick is to find their natural shoaling areas and get them accustomed to a particular bait. In some instances this is done for you. I recall a harbour in southern Ireland where the local creamery pumped its waste milk products straight into the sea. It was only necessary to take up a position close to the outfall, bait up with a tiny portion of cream cheese and start hauling in the fish. This was the only place I ever found mullet 'easy'. Everywhere else required patience, stealth and ultra-fine tackle.

Despite their cunning, mullet will accept a multitude of baits. Worm, maggot, cheese, bread, cooked macaroni, tinned peas, banana and raw meat have all been used successfully. Basically a summer species, mullet appear in late May or early June and stay round the southern half of mainland Britain until early October. They then head offshore, appearing round the Channel Islands in late November. I have never caught mullet north of the Thames estuary, but south of this point they are a very common species. We have seen that mullet can be caught on float tackle or baited spinner. Occasionally, however, they will accept a bait on a light paternoster rig (see Fig. 37). This set-up is ideal for use on piers or jetties where the mullet browse round the iron or stonework. To fish effectively the angler has to fish straight up and down, watching the rod top for any indication of a bite. A better technique is to use a quivertip rod, the ultra-soft, fine tip giving a clear indication the moment a mullet samples the bait.

Mullet are thought of as a calm-water fish, harbours and estuaries being

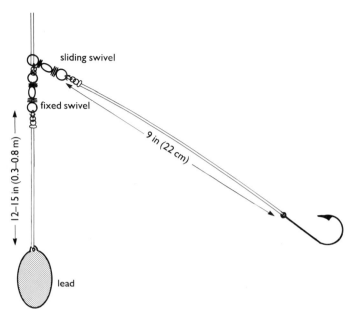

FIGURE 37   A paternoster can be used successfully when the fish are feeding too deep for float tackle.

FIGURE 38   A mullet spinner.

typical mullet strongholds. But not all mullet adhere to the rules. On Cornwall's Atlantic coast, where the swells turn the rock gullies into a maelstrom of white water, these fish can often be taken in quantity. This is not light-tackle country, and the wise angler uses a hefty rod, large floats and lines of 18–20 lb (8.2–9.1 kg) breaking strain. This is crude gear by most mullet-fishing standards but essential in an area where it is necessary to swing each hooked fish up onto a high rock ledge. I was introduced many years ago to the Sennen Cove style of mullet fishing. My instructor was an ancient Cornishman who knew the habits of the local mullet well. The shirvy was mashed bread mixed with pilchard oil, and the hook bait was a chunk of flake from a newly baked loaf. It took several trips to convince me that mullet would live and feed in the sort of white water I normally associated with bass. I watched my tutor take big bags of moderate mullet of 1½–2½ lb (0.7–1.1 kg). Once I got over my uncertainty about the place and methods, I too started to catch fish. Later I branched out and caught many good bags of fish from other north Cornish venues.

Many anglers still regard mullet as totally uncatchable. For this reason many good mullet-holding areas never get fished. This is a pity, for big mullet fight harder than bass of similar size. Moreover, mullet are normally encountered in huge shoals. Catch one and you should catch others. I have proved to my own satisfaction that I can catch mullet in a variety of ways, and this has led me to try for them in unfished areas. In some places I have had several blank trips before finding the right technique, but if anything this has added to the eventual satisfaction of taking good fish.

10

Pollack and Coalfish

Of all the medium-weight sea fish the angler can hope to catch, pollack and coalfish are among the gamest. Hooked in deep water, a big fish of either species can make a dive for cover at unbelievable speed. The largest specimens of both species are normally found offshore over reefs and deep-sunk wrecks. For many years the wrecks off Devon and Cornwall produced the best catches of pollack and coalfish. Recently, however, free-thinking charter-boat skippers have begun wreck fishing off Hampshire and Sussex. These newer wreck marks have produced vast catches of big pollack. For example, Roger Bayzand, skipper of the Lymington boat *Sundance II*, recently brought in a catch of 153 big pollack from a single day's fishing. Coalfish have yet to establish themselves on the up-Channel wrecks. Even so, a few 'coalies' are being caught and it looks as though this magnificent fish will in time colonize such marks.

Of the two species pollack are probably the more common and more widely distributed. I have caught good pollack from the English Channel, from Scotland and Orkney and from both Northern Ireland and the south of Ireland. On rocky coastlines it is possible to catch pollack of well over 10 lb (4.5 kg) from the shore. These large fish are basically nocturnal, rarely showing up during daylight. A live pouting or, better still, a sand eel, fished at night under a float can work wonders. An inshore pollack of over 10 lb (4.5 kg) hits a livebait like a runaway train. Such 'smash' takes are hard to miss on the strike. In Scotland, where coalfish are common, the inshore specimens rarely weigh more than about 2 lb (0.9 kg), but these give excellent sport on light float or spinning gear. The larger specimens invariably come from deep water. Wrecks sunk in 35–50 fathoms (64–91 m) are the ideal place to locate big coalfish. In West Country waters these big fish are most common during the winter.

Very much a shoaling fish, coalfish, particularly the smaller specimens, can often be taken like mackerel. I recall one day off Orkney when we stopped to feather mackerel for skate bait. Instead of mackerel we hit coalfish of 3–5 lb (1.4–2.3 kg). Six coalfish at one time take some handling and it was not long before every angler on the boat had snipped three feathers off his line to make life more bearable. Finally, we gave up. No matter where we stopped, it was coalfish, with not a single mackerel caught. Later that day I used one of the smaller coalfish to catch a skate of 192 lb (87 kg). The next day coalfish gave me a second monster, this time 158 lb (72 kg)

TACKLE

For float fishing or spinning from the shore or harbour walls I find that the perfect combination is a 10 ft (3 m) carbon carp rod with a Shimano Aero fixed-spool reel. This reel has a tournament-style spool designed for ultra-long casting. It also incorporates a sophisticated stern drag system which makes playing a fish a true pleasure. Many modern reels have this system, but I find those from Shimano hard to equal. This rod and reel combination has the power to control a hefty fish yet is light enough to cast small baits and to hold comfortably all day. For boat work I use a 20 lb (9.1 kg) class boat rod fitted with a Shimano TLD 20 lever drag reel. At a pinch any 4–0 multiplying reel can be used, but again I prefer the drag system and extremely smooth power of the TLD 20.

Pollack and coalfish both turn on the power the second they feel the hook. For this reason, only the best tackle should be used. Unaccountably, many sea anglers spend a lot of money on a rod and reel, then spoil the combination by using cheap line and hooks. This can only lead to lost fish. When a big coalfish or pollack turns for home it takes maximum pressure to stop it. Use cheap line and poor hooks and you can say goodbye to seven out of every ten fish you hook.

METHODS

Trolling

For anglers fortunate enough to live in an area where a rocky coastline falls away into deep water the most productive way to catch pollack and the occasional coalfish is to troll an artificial lure close in to the rocky cliffs. For this style of angling the 20 lb (9.1 kg) class boat outfit should be used. The terminal tackle is simple: tie a 4–8 oz (115–225 g) or, if necessary, a 10 oz (280 g) banana lead (see Fig. 39) to the end of the reel line. This lead normally has a barrel swivel attached to one end. Tie 3 yards (2.7 m) of 30 lb (13.6 kg) nylon to the swivel and then fix the artificial lure of your choice to the other end of the nylon. Plugs, spoons and rubber eels can all be used for trolling. The artificial sand eel known as a Red Gill is the best bait. These are available in a variety of colours, and it pays to carry a selection. One day black may be the killing colour, the next it may be red, or blue and silver. (See Fig. 39 and Fig. 43)

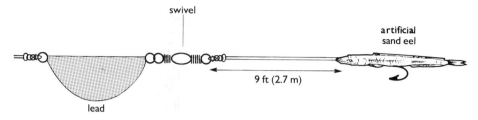

swivel

artificial
sand eel

9 ft (2.7 m)

lead

FIGURE 39   A banana-shaped lead is needed for trolling. Experiment with distances. It is hard to predict how deep and how far behind the boat pollack or bass will feed.

POLLACK

These beautiful fish provide superb sport on light tackle, and on offshore grounds, particularly round reefs and wrecks, they grow to a large size. Pollack are an Atlantic species and the largest nearly all come from West Country waters. Good-sized pollack are rarely found over sandy ground; the best marks are almost always very rocky, tall underwater pinnacles and large, sunken reefs being ideal. In recent years wreck fishing has accounted for huge catches of pollack, most falling to artificial baits.

Pollack move from one ground to another. In May and June they hug the pinnacles as closely as possible. Later they move further out and feed over rough and stony ground, within easy reach of the main rocky outcrops. In late autumn, however, pollack become wanderers and will turn up almost any-where. Big pollack are almost always found in deep water, whereas the smaller fish usually congregate on top of a reef or pinnacle. In late autumn and early winter big pollack often move inshore in large numbers. This shoreward migration also occurs off the Irish coast.

Since wreck fishing began in earnest, the original pollack record has been smashed many times. A 16 lb (7.3 kg) pollack was at one time regarded as a huge specimen, but in recent years a fish has needed to weigh 20 lb (9.1 kg) to be noteworthy.

Pollack and coalfish frequent similar areas. This angler took a mixed brace of pollack on pirk and coalfish on plastic squid.

COALFISH

The coalfish is similar to the pollack in appearance. The easiest way of telling the two apart is by comparing the lower jaw: if it projects well beyond the upper jaw, the fish is a pollack; if it recedes or is the same length as the upper jaw, it is a coalfish. The lateral lines of the two species also differ. The pollack's is dark on a light background, while that of the coalfish is light on a dark background. The species also vary considerably in colour from one locality to another, the brightest-coloured fish usually coming from fairly shallow water. These are a burnished gold in colour, with white or off-white bellies. Deep-water coalfish are usually greyish-green, with white underparts. Coalfish are generally rather darker than pollack, but light-coloured specimens occur in many areas. Although big coalfish have quite a girth, they invariably have a long, rakish appearance. Active hunters, they are capable of sudden bursts of terrific speed.

Coalfish have a wide distribution, but are commonest in northern waters. They grow to a larger size than pollack, the record for the species currently standing at over 33 lb (15 kg). In Scottish waters, huge shoals of coalfish of up to 5 lb (2.3 kg) can often be encountered close to the shore. The larger specimens, however, seldom venture inshore of the 15–20 fathom (27–37 m) line.

I remember fishing a section of Orkney's rugged coastline that promised excellent pollack sport. I tried all the usual coloured Red Gills without a sign of a fish. Finally, I came across a dull purple eel which I had never used. It was a case of nothing ventured, nothing gained, but I did not hold out much hope for the purple eel. Obviously, though, that lure had something that the fish wanted. On the first drop I had a 12-pounder (5.4 kg) and ten minutes later a fish of 14 lb (6.3 kg). Then I lost the eel on a rocky ledge. I tried every other eel that I had, but to no avail. The fish wanted only that one totally unnatural and unattractive colour. The next time, blue and silver produced a bumper catch.

For trolling the rod should be held at all times. Put it down and a taking fish will snatch it straight out of the boat. I like to fish with the reel set on a light drag. I use the ball of my right thumb to brake the reel spool. This enables me to set the hook yet still have a drag setting that allows a big fish to take a little line. If the drag is set too tightly, the chances are that a striking fish will hit the lure with such an impact that the 20 lb (9.1 kg) reel line will snap.

Wreck fishing

On occasion, wreck pollack and coalfish will happily pick up a jigged pirk or a natural fish bait. But the best rig yet devised to catch them in quantity is a Red Gill or Eddystone eel on a flying collar (see Fig. 40). The extra-long wire boom is used to stop the lure from wrapping round the reel line during its long drop down to the wreck. Once the lead touches bottom, wind in to a fast count of fifty, and I mean fast. The artificial eel has to come out of the wreck as though its tail is on fire. If a fish has not nailed the lure by the time fifty is reached, send the tackle back down and start again.

When a strike does come, it is like hitting a solid obstruction that suddenly comes to life and powers back towards the wreck. A big coalfish is particularly adept at racing for sanctuary. Once a fish is hooked it must be strongarmed away from its objective. Allow it to get to the wreck and a breakage is inevitable. After more than 20 years of intensive wreck fishing I am still amazed at the turn of speed a pollack or coalfish can summon up during the early stages of the battle. Once the fish is up to the mid-water mark it usually gives up. But below this depth it is a capable and very active fighter.

Reef fishing

A nice way of catching reef pollack is to fish with the carp rod and small fresh-water multiplier. The terminal tackle consists of a fixed lead, a 10 ft (3.3 m) trace and a size 2–0 hook baited with a live or dead sand eel or king ragworm. The technique is simple: the baited tackle is lowered to the reef, then slowly wound up so that the eel or worm appears to swim lazily towards the surface. To a hunting pollack a bait which behaves in this manner must appear totally natural. The fish simply follow the bait for a short distance, then slide gently up and engulf it. Bites are often mere nibbles rather than rod-slamming wallop. By using this technique it is often possible to take a better than average bag of medium weight fish.

Drift lining

This is a technique similar to that of reef fishing. With the driftline only the minimum amount of lead should be used. The bait is live sand eel. The boat should be anchored up-tide of a reef (see Fig. 41) and the bait allowed to swim naturally with the flow of the tide. For this style of fishing a light fine-wire size 1 or 1–0 Aberdeen hook should be passed through the eel's mouth and out of the gill slit. The point of the hook is then nicked lightly through the skin of the bait's belly (see Fig. 42). Lightness is the key to this style of fishing. The biggest sand eel

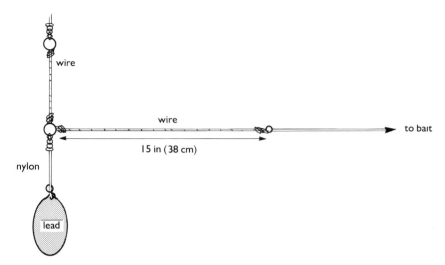

FIGURE 40   A typical rig. Use a short length of nylon to attach the lead.

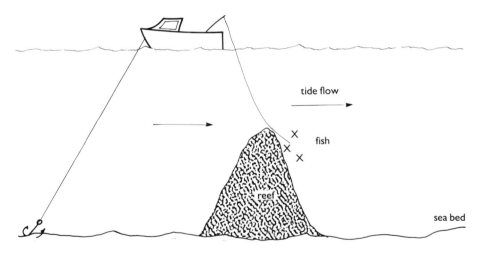

FIGURE 41   Fishing up-tide of a reef.

FIGURE 42   A sand eel hooked through belly skin.

is a light, fragile little fish. Additional weight simply stops it swimming naturally and often frightens away the highly observant pollack. Fished correctly, however, a drift-lined sand eel is deadly.

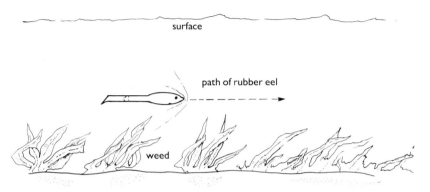

FIGURE 43   An artificial bait should also be worked above the weed line. Move the rod from side to side to add life to the bait.

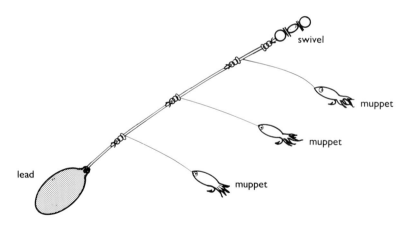

FIGURE 44   A 'muppet' rig made up of three plastic squid fished above a lead. This can prove a deadly set-up.

Float fishing

Pollack and coalfish are not basically bottom feeders. They work on the smash and grab principle, often covering a lot of ground during the course of a day's hunting. For this reason a 'muppet' rig works, while float fishing with worm, eel or a fish strip can also be highly productive. Streamlined sliding floats of the type sold for pike fishing are better than the traditionally over-heavy sea-style floats. The float should be set to fish the bait 1–2 ft (0.3–0.6 m) below the mid-water mark (e.g. if the water is around 20 ft (6 m) deep the bait should be fished at 12–14 ft (3.6–4.2 m)). A tiny section of rubber band tied to the reel line stops the float. When a pollack takes the bait the float usually shoots under at high speed. The strike must be made the instant the float disappears, for both pollack and inshore coalfish are adept at ejecting a suspect bait.

Bottom fishing

During autumn and winter some pollack forsake their traditional strongholds and move out to scavenge over open ground more suited to cod. At such times they can be caught on running leger baited with fish or squid, although usually more by accident than intent.

11

Skate and Ray

Ranging in weight from 4 lb (1.8 kg) to over 200 lb (91 kg), the various members of the skate and ray tribe offer good fishing for boat and, to a lesser extent, shore anglers. All species are bottom feeders, taking a variety of baits on running leger tackle. For many anglers a giant common skate is the fish of a lifetime. Many groups now book skate-fishing holidays in the hope of getting to grips with a fish of over 100 lb (45 kg). The lucky few catch a fish of double this weight. Below, the various species are described separately.

COMMON SKATE

Once common round the whole of Britain and Ireland, giant common skate are now confined to certain areas. The west coast of Scotland, Orkney and the Shetlands on the east, Northern Ireland and south-west Ireland offer the best chances of success. At present the most productive big-skate grounds are off Tobermory on the Isle of Mull. Here local skipper Brian Swinbanks has made a science of big skate fishing. His practice of total conservation has shown the angling world that skate stocks can be maintained as long as a policy of catch, weigh, and release is adhered to. Brian has fitted a gantry to his boat. Fish are gaffed in the wing, lifted inboard, weighed, photographed and swung back out and lowered gently into the sea. Many released skate have been caught again. More important still, released fish live to breed in future seasons. In areas where each rod-caught skate was automatically killed, giant skate have vanished, wiped out by ignorance and self-gratification. Most long-term boat anglers have been guilty of killing fish. Most of us now realize, far too late, that we were wrong to bring in such trophy fish. Take my own area off the Isle of Wight. When I first fished south of the Needles lighthouse, giant skate were fairly common. The top mark was the legendary Pot Bank, now dredged out of existence. Another favourite hole was under Tennyson's monument, Freshwater

Bay. Here there was a mud gully which was once a big-skate hotspot. Unusually, both areas were subject to heavy runs of tide. This is unusual, for big skate are lazy fish, preferring to live and wait for their food in slackish water on the edge of the main tide flow.

I remember a big-skate expedition in late August. It was a long-planned trip and we had a couple of journalists on board. The plan was to fish overnight for skate then up anchor at dawn and move offshore to try for a shark. It was one of those warm, dark nights and I was hopeful. During the past week I had caught two skate weighing 95 and 100 lb (43 and 45 kg) from the mark. Now I hoped for something larger. The previous season a Yarmouth, Isle of Wight boat had caught a 139 lb (63 kg) skate in the area. Tonight I thought we might top 150 lb (68 kg). Fishing with me was Dave Fawcett, from Lymington, a good angler with many big fish to his credit. From 8 until 11 pm nothing much happened. Twice we had changed baits and now, with the slack-water period finished, my earlier optimism was beginning to wane. The tide rips through this area at high speed. Earlier fish had all come at dead slack water. Still, we were out for the night, so we fished on.

At 11.15 Dave reported a bite. Nothing hard, though, just a gentle dipping of the rod tip. Several minutes went by and he said the line had gone slack. I knew then that a big skate had taken his half mackerel. Every big one I had caught or seen caught had taken the bait and moved up-tide, creating a slack line. Quickly putting him in the picture, I suggested he wind in the slack until he felt the weight of the running fish. Seconds later he made positive contact. The heavy glass rod lurched down as the fish felt the drag. Most big skate dig in the second they realize they are in trouble. But not this one, and instead of using its vast body as a suction disc it surged off up-tide. This was dangerous. The line was practically

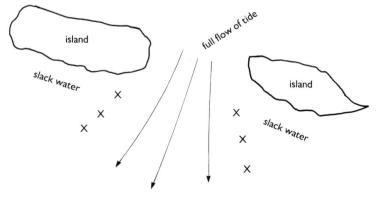

X = giant skate

FIGURE 45 Giant skate often prefer slacker water at the edge of a run of tide, where the flow can provide a plentiful supply of food. A gap between islands provides an ideal site.

under our keel and if the fish kept going the chances were that it would foul the anchor cable. Urging Dave to apply maximum pressure, I waited to see whether the fish would turn. Fortunately, it did. The combination of heavy rod, big reel and 80 lb (36.2 kg) line was sufficient to divert the fish. Slowly it 'kited' round in the tide, then changed gear and shot off in the opposite direction. After a 60 yard (55 m) dash it hit bottom and stuck itself down firmly. Once again Dave exerted maximum pressure, at first to no avail. Finally, however, the fish shifted slightly. As it did so Dave forced it up, and once again it was on the move.

Two hours later the situation was exactly the same: the fish would stick to the bottom, rise up again and plug round slowly and steadily. The tide was now raging and this gave the fish a great deal of help. Twice it was up to the surface, only to crash dive into deep, dark water. In all, it fought for four hours and fifty-five painful minutes. We were all convinced it was a monster, right to the last. Then I gaffed it. A second gaff was used and as we dragged it into the boat I was disappointed to see that it was not as big as I had thought. It was over the magic 100 lb (45 kg) mark, but not by much. How could a fish of this size fight so long and so hard? I soon found out when I came to unhook it. Instead of being in its mouth, the hook was stuck in the outside edge of the huge fish. With the fish foulhooked in this way, little or no real rod pressure could be applied. In those days fish like this were kept. Later, it weighed in at 110 lb (50 kg) – no monster, but it had done so much damage to the muscles of Dave's forearms that they had to be strapped up for several weeks. This was one of the last giant skate caught off the island. The dredgers ruined the once-great Pot Bank and we anglers ruined the only other mark used by the skate.

To grow to a weight of over 100 lb (45 kg) takes a skate 30 or more years. Fish of double this weight are thought to be 60 or 70 years old. The largest skate I have caught weighed 192 lb (87 kg). This was an Orkney giant skate caught while fishing out from Kirkwall; a typical fish that came from a food-rich, slack-water area close to a main flow of tide. I was out with Kirkwall boatman Eddie

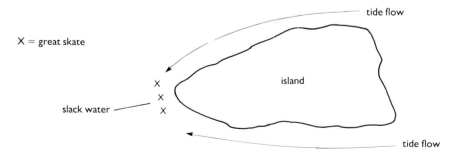

FIGURE 46 A typical giant skate habitat. A tidal flow split by an island provides a slack area for skate to congregate.

Sinclair. The ground we intended to fish was a known scallop mark where local scallop divers had reported seeing giant common skate. Big skate tend to feed on scallops, and extensive scallop beds are a common factor in locating them. On this trip we had stopped close to a rocky island to feather a dozen or so small coalfish. We could have caught mackerel but northern skate much prefer fresh coalfish.

To get the best out of coalfish each bait should be partially filleted. The whole coalfish should be laid on a bait board, then cut from tail to head. The bait is turned over and the procedure repeated. The back bone is then chopped out and discarded. This leaves a swallow-tailed bait held together by the head (see Fig. 47). To present this bait properly the hook should be passed through both of its eye sockets. This gives a good, firm hook hold and yet allows the bait to waver in the tide flow. Because the bait is half filleted, the body juices seep out, laying a strong scent trail. Large skate hunt by scent, sight and vibration. Once they lock onto a scent they follow it back to source.

To return to our Scottish trip, we were fishing in 120 ft (37 m) of water and, as usual, the boat was anchored. I was using my favourite outfit for skate, a 50 lb (22.6 kg) class rod matched with a multiplier holding a minimum of 220 yards (200 m) of 50 lb (22.6 kg) nylon. On this occasion I had chosen an American rod

---

COMMON SKATE

Common skate – sometimes known as grey or blue skate – grow to huge weights. Specimens of up to 150 lb (68 kg) are still fairly common, and fish of over 200 lb (91 kg) are known to exist in many places off the coast of Britain and Ireland. Under favourable conditions skate reach weights of over 300 lb (136 kg), while one commercially caught fish weighed in at 400 lb (181 kg) and was over 7 ft (2.1 m) long. Although technically not a true big-game species, giant skate are large and powerful enough to attract the attention of many big-fish anglers.

Skate, like most big fish, tend to pick out a small section of food-rich sea bed and take up permanent residence there. Although skate are not a shoal fish, a number of individual specimens may live in close harmony. This often makes it possible to catch several skate in a day's fishing.

A big skate will eat almost anything edible it comes across. Examination of the stomach contents of the large common skate I have caught has produced the remains of crabs, lobsters, dogfish, pouting, mackerel and even small skate – proof that a big skate has a large and varied diet.

FIGURE 47 A flapper skate bait. Do not strike at the first indication of a bite; the initial pull is not a bite at all, it is the skate flopping down on top of bait and line.

and a Tatler V reel; a good outfit, but now dated. For future skate trips I have obtained a 50 lb (22.6 kg) class carbon/fibreglass rod and a Shimano TLD 25 lever drag reel, one of the best reel currently available. A big fish will show up any defect in tackle. This is particularly true of reel spools, which can distort under the crushing power of contracting nylon line. The TLD 25 has been tested on some of the world's hardest-fighting fish. This makes it perfect for skate fishing.

One of the most important parts of a skate outfit is the trace. Giant skate do not have teeth but their lips are heavily armoured with sharp-edged scale-like plates. These, coupled with the immense power generated by the skate's jaw muscles, can crush and chafe through heavy scallop or crab shell. I make my traces from 150 lb (68 kg) long-liners' nylon, each being 39 in (1 m) long. For extra strength I knot and crimp both the hook and the swivel in place. Heavy nylon has more resistance than nylon-covered wire. In theory the nylon sheath is there to protect the wire core. Unfortunately, this sheath often catches on the skate's lip plates. Once damaged, the nylon may snag on a plate, allowing the fish to saw away at the wire core. Heavy-duty nylon does not suffer from this problem.

On the day I caught the 192-pounder (87 kg) I had just one bite. The fish came at slack water and, predictably, moved up towards the boat with the bait in its mouth. Once hooked, it flopped down hard on the sea bed, at first refusing to budge. Applied rod pressure soon forced its snout up and from that time on it fought a hard, running, diving battle. Finally it was gaffed, but we nearly lost it. The gaff head straightened and the great fish dropped back into the sea. Somehow I managed to keep it on the surface, although I was forced to give line. Eddie saved the day by slipping the anchor rope, allowing the boat to drift back to the fish. This time there was no mistake. As Eddie sank the first gaff, I laid down the rod and placed a second gaff securely into the fish's wing. The next day I caught another 'biggie', a 158-pounder (72 kg), in Scapa Flow from a Stromness boat. This second fish likewise fell to a partially filleted coalfish.

To stand a good chance of catching a skate of over 100 lb (45 kg) you have to go to the fish. I have already mentioned the hotspots on both sides of Scotland. In addition, Strangford and Carlingford loughs, in Northern Ireland, are the strongholds of big skate. In the south of Ireland many formerly prolific big-skate grounds are now lifeless. Overfishing has taken its toll but there are still one or two places left in the south west of Ireland where big skate can be taken. The Irish are now very committed to conserving their fish stocks, and this policy could in time help the skate to re-establish itself in many of its old haunts.

STING RAY

Although much smaller than the common skate, the sting ray can exceed 60 lb (27.2 kg). Very much an inshore species, it is a lover of muddy, shallow waters. It is common over the Thames and Essex mud flats and also in the margins of the Solent. Most rod-caught sting ray fall to beach or inshore dinghy anglers, the average size of such fish ranging from 10 to 40 lb (4.5–18.1 kg). The usual baits for this species are ragworm and hermit or peeler crab. Sting ray of over 40 lb (18.1 kg) often forsake their traditional homes and move out into deep water, and in doing so also change their feeding habits. Squid and fish fillets have accounted for some huge sting ray in unexpected places.

The largest British sting ray I have caught came on a dark, sultry night over a typical piece of rugged conger ground. This fish would normally have been returned, but a member of the charter party wanted to try and eat it. When the fish had been gutted, the remaining pair of wings weighed 44 lb (20 kg). Intact, the fish probably weighed over 50 lb (22.6 kg). A 58½ lb (26.5 kg) specimen was taken the same year from a Sussex deep-water mark. Others of comparable size have turned up in similar locations. It is possible that fish of above average weight are unable to find sufficient food in shallow water, and that hunger drives them offshore to feed on alien ground.

Most sting ray are caught by shore anglers using standard beach-casting equipment. This comprises a 12 ft (3.6 m) beach caster, a multiplying reel loaded with 18 lb (8.2 kg) nylon and a standard running leger rig baited with worm or crab. As always, a 30 ft (9 m) shock leader of 30 lb (13.6 kg) nylon should be added between the reel line and the terminal tackle. Most stingray anglers use a pair of rods, as this allows two types of bait to be used and doubles the chance of success. Sting ray are seldom caught in quantity. The rods are normally propped in a rest with the reel on ratchet. 'Stingers' are not shy biting and the ratchet gives audible warning when a fish picks up the bait. They are active fish capable of putting up a good fight, and on occasion a hooked fish may even try to jump. No other skate or ray attempts this manoeuvre.

Once played out and ready for beaching, the ray should be handled with great care, for it has a habit of flailing its whip-like tail about at high speed. The tail is armed with a long multi-barbed spine which can drive straight through waders.

STING RAY

Sting ray are very similar in shape to skate, but have a rounder outline. They are normally a drab brown, without spots or blotches, and have mottled whitish-grey underparts. The body is covered in a layer of thick, evil-smelling slime. The species gets its name from its long, whip-like tail, the jagged, bony spine of which can inflict a serious wound. This spine is grooved and carries a venom which can cause intense pain and even temporary paralysis.

Sting ray are a summer species and the best months to try for them are June and July, when they are found in shallow waters. It is generally believed that they migrate offshore for the winter. However, I think that they probably spend the winter months in hibernation.

Although I have known sting ray to take fish baits, their favourite food is lugworm and ragworm. They also feed on crabs and shellfish.

Moreover, the slime on the spine will infect any cut it comes into contact with. To avoid such an accident it is advisable to carry a small piece of 3 in (7.5 cm) board, which can be dropped over the tail and stood on while the fish is unhooked. At one time anglers unnecessarily chopped off the ray's tail. Fortunately, today's anglers handle the fish with caution, but return it alive and intact to the sea.

BLONDE RAY AND UNDULATE RAY

Both of these beautiful fish are lovers of strong tides. Most ray prefer to exist on the edge of a tide flow, but these two varieties are normally found below the lip of banks which are swept by savage tidal flows. Typical blonde ray strongholds are the Shambles, off Weymouth, the Skerries Bank and Lannacombe Bay off Dartmouth and the offshore banks of the Channel Islands. The undulate ray is even more localized, and is common only in certain areas round the Channel Islands. However, it is found in considerable numbers off Tralee Bay, Co. Kerry, in Ireland.

The blonde ray is the larger of the two species, reaching weights of over 35 lb (15.9 kg). The undulate reaches a maximum weight of around 20 lb (9.1 kg). The coloration of the undulate is more dramatic than that of the blonde ray. Sometimes called the painted or popart ray, it has a basically sandy-coloured back that is highlighted by a series of dark lines and blotches. When freshly caught it is a vivid, unmistakable fish. In recent seasons an increasing number of

BLONDE RAY

The blonde ray is less angular than the thornback and lacks its large, thorn-like spines. It is usually sandy-coloured on the back, with a thick sprinkling of small black spots extending to the margins of the wings. There are also nine or ten pale roundels on the body disc. The underparts are white. Blonde ray grow on average to a greater size than thornback, but are seldom caught in any quantity. Sadly, a real record-breaker of nearly 40 lb (18.1 kg) was eaten before its captor realized what a monster he had boated. The species is common in the English Channel and on the Atlantic coast, but seems to be rather rare in the North Sea.

Hermit crab are a favourite food of the blonde ray, although most of the fish caught on rod and line fall to fish-fillet baits of various types.

undulate ray have been caught round the Isle of Wight, an area where they were once unknown. Both species take up a position either on the downward slope or in the actual trough at the bottom of the bank. Here they can obtain sand eel, but they will take other small fish or fish cuttings. A favourite bait is a belly fillet (see Fig. 48). from a fresh mackerel. This strip looks very similar to a sand eel and is a highly effective substitute. Owing to their love of rough water, these rays are often fished for with wire line (see page 25).

When wire line was first introduced into Britain I was asked to test its potential. For one of the first trials I fished the Shambles. Notorious for its heavy tides and big fish, this bank seemed an ideal test site. The object of wire line was to cut through the tide flow and allow the use of far smaller weights than conventional lines would allow. Regulars on the Shambles used leads of up to 4 lb (1.8 kg). Now, with wire, we hoped to use a maximum weight of 1½ lb (0.7 kg). It worked like a dream. I had planned the day with Weymouth clubman Jim Churchhouse and friends, and they were instantly taken with the potential of wire. To begin with, we had several nice turbot and a few medium-size blonde ray, and the wire was behaving perfectly. Most important of all, it actually allowed me to search out fish on the downward slope of the bank, as the lead

FIGURE 48   A mackerel belly fillet cut to the outline of a sand eel.

held its place until it was lifted and dropped back. With standard nylon or Dacron lines this was practically impossible to achieve. Furthermore, each bite was clearly discernible.

As slack water approached I was down to 12 oz (340 g) of lead, whereas the Weymouth anglers still had to use 2 lb (0.9 kg) or more to stand a chance holding the bait down. It was at this stage that I felt a slight trembling tap on the rod tip. My initial impression was that a pout or similar small fish had tried to take the big bait. For several moments nothing else happened, then suddenly the rod was practically torn from my hands, the fish hooking itself in the process. The moment it moved I knew it was a blonde ray, and a big one. Even at slack water the tide over the Shambles runs at a good speed and the fish know just how to get the best out of the prevailing water pressure. Three times I was able to work the fish towards the boat only to lose line again as the struggling ray 'kited' up, using its broad, flat body as a drogue. A ray that adopts such tactics can be a difficult fish to boat. Being new to wire-line fishing, I had no idea how the single strand, or stell, would stand up to such brutal work. As time passed, however, my confidence grew, giving me the nerve to pile on additional rod pressure. Finally, these tactics started to pay off.

I had the fish on the move and each precious yard of line I gained stayed on the reel spool. At last, I had the ray on the surface, and the trace swivel was actually out of the water. With less than 10 yards (9 m) to go I was certain of boating the fish, which was now in clear view. I had seen the three previous record blonde ray, but this fish looked bigger, much bigger. The boat skipper was at that time the holder of the record and his opinion was the same as mine: it definitely looked like a 40 lb-plus (18.1 kg) fish. I stepped up the pressure, intent on gaining those few vital yards. Then, all of a sudden, the trace material snapped. The 40 lb (19.1 kg) wire had held but the nylon of the same breaking strain had parted below the joining swivel. The ray vanished instantly. My only consolation was that the lead and Kilmore boom would have come off the trace instantly, so that the fish simply had a hook and a short length of nylon to drag about. I have never caught a blonde ray anywhere near the size of that fish. Off Alderney I took a 29½ pounder (13.3 kg), but so far I cannot break the 30 lb (13.6 kg) barrier.

Undulate ray are different. I have caught scores of specimens, all from marks in southern Ireland. At one time I used to make an annual pilgrimage to Fenit, in Co. Kerry. From here I was able to go out daily to fish the whole of Tralee Bay and round the Maharee Islands. The ray fishing in this area is phenomenal and the undulate ray, which is rare elsewhere, is the most common local species. An added attraction was that we also caught monkfish, tope and on one occasion two 100 lb-plus (45 kg) skate. The local bait was mackerel fillet. I discovered, however, that if I used a match rod, a light line and a tiny float, Fenit pier would

Big blonde ray like this magnificent 25-pounder (11.4 kg) are normally caught over ground washed by heavy tides. This fish was taken on a fillet of fresh mackerel.

produce endless sand smelt; beauties of 4 and 5 in (10 and 12.5 cm) reeking with a cucumber-like smell. These freshly caught deadbaits were lethal. Fished on standard running leger and a size 4–0 hook, they would outcatch a mackerel bait by a ratio of three to one. Once their effectiveness was known, every angler in the area descended on the pier to catch bait for the following day. Fortunately, the smelt were so numerous that no matter how many were taken there were still plenty left.

I recall that in one week's fishing six of us caught over 200 undulate ray, most of them weighing 12–15 lb (5.4–6.8 kg). All were returned alive to the water. Like the blonde ray, the undulate is a fighter, using the tide to good effect. It is several years since I last visited Fenit but the undulate were at that time still being taken in quantity – proof of the benefits to sea angling of conservation. Long may this progress continue, as more and more thinking anglers come into the sport.

THORNBACK RAY

As its name implies, the thornback ray carries a number of thorn-like spines on its back and tail. These can be very sharp and to avoid injury it is essential to handle the fish carefully. It is best to use a gardening glove or an old towel to pick up the fish.

Rod catches indicate that thornback travel in small groups, each comprising one large female and a number of attendant males. Usually the female is the first to get caught, the males following in quick succession. Like all skate, thornback are caught hard on the bottom using a single-hook running leger. The bait is normally fish strip or squid, and shore anglers may also use bunched black lugworm. For boat fishing a small attractor spoon (see Fig. 49) can be a useful addition to the terminal tackle. Light plastic flounder spoon blades make good thornback attractors. A standard 30 lb (13.6 kg) class boat fishing rod and reel is perfect for thornback fishing. These fish also respond well to up-tide casting methods.

To catch thornback consistently it is essential to use enough lead to keep the bait in an anchored position no matter what strength of tide is encountered. A bait that trots or rolls over the sea bed may catch cod and other free-swimming predators, but will seldom catch ray. For the same reason the trace should have a maximum length of 2 ft (0.6 m), for a bait that is lifted by the tide holds little appeal to thornback. When a bite is detected it must be left to develop. A thornback's mouth is situated on the underside of its body and when the fish first flops onto a bait its wings give a false indication. Strike at this and you will either foulhook the fish or whip the bait out from under it. Once alarmed, the fish will vacate the area.

FIGURE 49   An attractor spoon fitted to leger tackle for thornback ray. It is probable that ray mistake the spoon blade for a small fish.

THORNBACK RAY

The thornback ray is variable in colour, but is usually brown or greyish-brown on the back. This basic colour is overlaid with pale spots surrounded by borders of small, dark spots. Smallish fish have banded tails, but the bands are often absent from large specimens. The underparts are white. Thornback grow to a fairly large size and specimens of nearly 40 lb (18.1 kg) have been taken. Most rod-caught thornback weigh 7–12 lb (3.2–5.4 kg), a 20 lb (9.1 kg) fish being regarded in most areas as a good catch.

The species has a wide distribution, being found in most places round the British Isles. Thornback are plentiful in the English Channel, and some of the Scottish sea lochs are thick with them. They are commonest where the sea bed is of sand, mud or gravel, although they are sometimes caught over rocks. The skate grounds off the Isle of Wight are often a mixture of rock and flat clay mud, and these areas produce larger-than-average thornback at most times of the year.

Thornback are generally regarded as a summer species, and often feed in fairly shallow water. In winter they move offshore on to the deeper marks. Like all the skate and rays, thornback are bottom feeders, and are adept at catching crustacea, worms and small fish.

Sometimes thornback ray are encountered in vast numbers. I once led a party for a week's fishing off the Isle of Mull. It was an experimental trip in early April, the aim being to establish whether or not the local marks would produce outside of the normal summer season. What we really wanted was giant common skate. What we got was a wealth of large thornback and two common skate. The hotspot was off Ardnamurchan Point. Fishing in water over 140 ft (43 m) deep we spent two days blitzing a never-ending stream of thornback. So engrossed were we that we forgot about catching a big skate and scaled down our tackle accordingly. If anything, our third day was turning out more productive than the previous two. Brian Swinbanks had moved out to slightly deeper water. The new mark was solid with ray. Pat Eldridge, who was using 40 lb (18.1 kg) wire line, was doing exceptionally well. He had caught and released at least ten thornback when he struck at what looked like a typical ray bite. It soon became obvious that this was a common skate and not a thornback ray. Forty-five minutes later it was in the boat, weighed and back in the sea. A good but not outstanding fish, it weighed 114 lb (52 kg). An examination of the tackle showed that the wire had sawed right through into the tip roller. A few seconds more and it would have fallen apart. The next day I boated and returned a 150 pounder (68 kg) on 30 lb (13.6 kg) line, again in a batch of thornback ray. There is evidence to show that large common skate actually eat small thornback. This may be why we caught big commons. Thornback ray infest deep estuaries, Cornwall's Fowey estuary being a good example. I can recall two of us catching 22 magnificent thornback while dinghy fishing there. The only bait these particular fish would take was live hard-backed crab. These were hooked through the eye sockets with a size 4–0 round-bend hook (see Fig. 50). Again, it was a matter of matching the bait to the natural food of the fish.

SMALL-EYED RAY

The small-eyed ray is now common along the south and south-west coastline of Britain. A decade or so ago, these fish were found in only a few locations. Since then, however, they have spread to many new areas. This colonization has included inshore as well as offshore areas, putting the small-eyed ray within reach of the beach and rock angler. Although never found far from a strong tidal flow, small-eyed ray like to live and feed out of the main force of water. Boat

FIGURE 50   A crab hooked through the channel behind its eye sockets.

anglers normally find them on the down-tide side of reefs and banks. When the tide changes the fish move over the bank to take advantage of the shelter. In deeper water small-eyed ray may feed throughout the hours of daylight. Inshore, however, they are essentially nocturnal feeders.

SMALL-EYED RAY

The small-eyed ray is similar in shape to the blonde ray, but is much paler. All those I have seen were a sandy colour on the back, with a series of pale spots and lines. The lines were most apparent on the extremities of the wings. The edges of the wings and the tail were outlined in brilliant white, which gave the fish a neat, clean appearance.

Small-eyed ray can be caught on standard skate/ray tackle, fished directly behind an anchored boat. Since the introduction of the up-tide casting technique it has been proved conclusively that a bait cast up and away from a boat produces far more action. The theory is that the fish shy away from the vibrations set up by the tide running past an anchor rope and under the keel. These vibrations set up a 'no go area' below and behind the boat. Casting in this way makes the bait drop into a vibration-free zone where the fish should be feeding without fear. Naturally, a boat-casting rod differs greatly from a standard boat rod. To gain distance the rod is 9 or 10 ft (2.7–3 m) long, and is of two sections of different length, the butt section being shorter than the tip. This staggered construction allows for long casts and yet leaves the tip light enough for instant bite detection. The up-tide casting rod is used with a small multiplying reel, the ABU 7000 and the new Shimano up-tide reel being the best.

The object of the up-tide method is to anchor the bait to the sea bed up-tide of the boat. To achieve this a very long, spiked lead is used, normally attached to a dropper tied directly to the trace swivel (see Fig. 51). The trace is usually 3–4 ft (0.9–1.2 m) in length. Hooks are kept small, a size 1–0 or 2–0 O'Shaughnessy being the best pattern. Specially designed up-tide hooks are also available. To aid casting, the baited hook is normally slipped over one of the lead spikes. Once the tackle hits the water the hook slides off the line and the bait hangs free. The long wire spikes on the lead are designed to dig into the sea bed. Once the lead is anchored the line should be tightened until the line between rod tip and lead is taut. When a fish picks up the bait it will dislodge the lead. Bites are then indicated by the rod springing back rather than pulling down. This is a small-bait method which can be extremely effective. The bait is normally a fish cutting or a small whole sand eel.

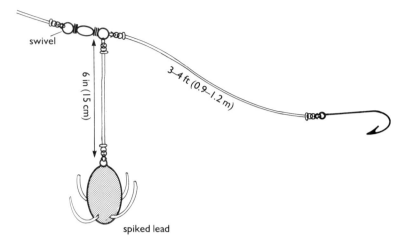

swivel

6 in (15 cm)

3–4 ft (0.9–1.2 m)

spiked lead

FIGURE 51   An up-tide lead tied to a dropper. Skate and ray are bottom feeders and move sluggishly across the sea bed.

For shore fishing a standard beach-casting outfit should be used. Small-eyed ray feed over sand shingle. Essentially a nocturnal species, small-eyed ray move inshore in search of small bait fish. In the West Country this means sand eel, and local anglers normally use fresh caught eels or, if necessary, blast-frozen eels. Further east, where sand eel are less common, small whole pouting or half pouting are the best bait. Quick to decompose, pouting are best caught as required and should always be used fresh. Most experienced south coast ray anglers carry and use a bait-catching rod. This is used with a three-hook paternoster rig baited with sections of ragworm or lugworm. Once it is completely dark, the bait rod should pick up a plentiful supply of small, bright pouting. Warm, sultry nights are good for small-eyed ray. Most beach anglers now adopt a policy of catch and release, ensuring sport for future seasons. The majority of shore-caught small-eyed ray weigh between 5 and 8 lb (2.3 and 3.6 kg). In the West Country, however, fish of 12–14 lb (5.4–6.3 kg) are caught.

CUCKOO AND SPOTTED RAY

These two pretty little ray seldom reach any size and so are rarely fished for. I have caught only one cuckoo ray in a lifetime's fishing, on a boat fishing expedition to Belfast Lough.

CUCKOO RAY

This fish is easy to identify, with its heart-shaped body and yellowish-brown back. To make identification even simpler, there is a large, dark eye-spot on each wing, with yellow spots and wavy lines superimposed on it. Cuckoo ray are widely distributed and, although not commonly caught, have been recorded in most parts of the British Isles. Most of the specimens taken have fallen to worm baits. Cuckoo ray are probably the smallest ray, and most weigh 1½–3 lb (0.7–1.4 kg).

SPOTTED RAY

The spotted ray is often confused with the blonde ray, for they have a basically similar appearance. However, the snout of the spotted variety is more prominent, and the overall colouring of its back is darker. Although pale spots are present on the spotted ray's back, they are less well defined than those on the blonde ray. There is often on each wing a single prominent pale blotch, which in every fish I have seen was bordered by a ring of small, dark spots.

Spotted ray are found all around the coast of the British Isles, generally in fairly shallow water. They are smaller than the blonde ray.

Spotted ray are more common than cuckoo ray and may grow to a weight of 5 lb (2.3 kg). Large spotted ray are often confused with young blonde ray (see box above).

Practically every spotted ray I have ever seen has had one pronounced pale spot on each of its wings. Invariably these pale blotches are bordered by a ring of dark spots. Normally a shallow-water species, spotted ray have a wide distribution. Like the cuckoo ray, they are normally caught on worm bait intended for flatfish.

12

Sea Bream

Both the black and the red sea bream were once far more common than they are now. The decline of these fish can be attributed to the rod and line angler rather than commercial fishing. Of the two, the black bream has suffered more. For many years shoals of these splendid fish arrived off the Sussex and Hampshire coastline intent only on spawning. Anglers and charter-boat skippers joined forces to harry them until many of the once-famous marks failed to produce fish. The famed Kingmere rocks, off the Sussex coast, are a good example of overfishing. From May to June anglers from all over the country flocked to Littlehampton to catch black bream in huge quantities. Finally, after many years of annual slaughter the bream shoals finally disappeared. It is possible, now that anglers adhere to self-imposed bag limits, that these delightful little fish will stage a comeback, perhaps even re-establishing themselves in something like their old numbers.

BLACK BREAM

The black bream, in particular, is an extremely popular light-tackle species, and few anglers use sea gear for it. They prefer a light fresh-water spinning rod and a fixed-spool or small multiplying reel. Wire strength is normally restricted to 6–7 lb (2.7–3.2 kg). Such an outfit is pleasant to use and is light enough to show up even the lightest of bream bites. Black bream have small mouths and so are best fished for with fresh-water hooks, a size 4 or 6 carp hook being ideal. Terminal tackle is a matter of personal preference. I like to keep my bait off the bottom and for this reason I use a single-hook paternoster incorporating a French boom (see Fig. 52), which has a 3 ft (0.9 m) nylon trace tied to it. Bream seem to like a bait that moves in the tide flow. The beauty of the French boom is that it can be adjusted instantly to change the depth of the bait. Many anglers prefer a long-link running leger made up with a long trace of 2 yards (1.8 m) or

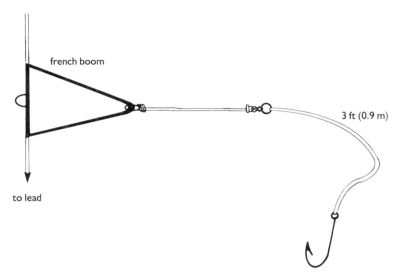

french boom

to lead

3 ft (0.9 m)

FIGURE 52   A simple running leger works well as terminal tackle, although a French boom does allow the trace to be lifted free of the lead. Sea bream fight well on light tackle.

more. This is also a good way of catching bream but more limited than the paternoster. In the days of plentiful bream, anglers used hinged bait droppers to lay a groundbait trail. These worked in a similar way to the bait distributor used by fresh-water float anglers. The hinged front panel was held in place by a length of wire which had a pendulum-like lead moulded to its end. The moment the lead touched bottom the impact would push the wire up to release the trap door. The groundbait would then wash out onto the bottom. Today, fish stocks are so low that such a device is seldom necessary.

One of the most effective bream groundbaits is cooked rice. Mixed bran and minced fish is also good. In the natural state black bream eat tiny fish, worms, crabs and brittle stars. This gives the angler a wide choice of bait. Ragworm, lugworm, slipper limpet, fish strip, and squid can all be used to good effect. Cocktail baits also appeal to bream. The first time I tried a cocktail bait was on a boat trip off Ballard Down, near Swanage, in Dorset. This area had always been noted for the quality of its bream fishing but over the years the fish had become decidedly finicky. Occasionally they would take a bait boldly, but mostly they would pick up a bait and drop it again instantly. On the day in question this was exactly what they were doing. Bites consisted of one light tap and nothing more. With six of us fishing, we had a wide variety of normally productive baits for the bream to choose from. None the less they refused to take properly, even though plenty of fish were clearly on the move. In desperation I decided to use a

SEA BREAM

The adult red bream is a deep-bodied fish. Its dorsal fin is long, well shaped and spiny, and its pectoral fins are elongated and sickle shaped. A mature red bream is orange-red, with silvery-pink sides. To make identification even easier, it has a distinctive black patch on its shoulder and very large eyes. An average-sized rod-caught red bream weighs 1½–2½ lb (0.7–1.1 kg), but fish of up to almost 8 lb (3.6 kg) have been taken.

Although red bream are beautiful fish to look at, they cannot compare for fighting spirit with black bream. The two varieties are similar in shape, but the pectoral fins are not as long in the black bream and, as the name implies, it is a dusky fish. The basic body colour is dark bluish-grey and the underparts are silvery white. Black bream that live on really rough ground often have dark vertical bands down their sides. Although black bream never reach the size of red bream, fish of 3–4 lb (1.4–1.8 kg) are common. Even a medium-sized black bream will put up a magnificent fight on all but the heaviest tackle.

The black bream's diet is similar to that of the red bream, and fish cuttings, worms and squid make the best baits. A mixture, such as squid and worm, is deadly. Combination baits of this kind often produce fish when conventional baits fail.

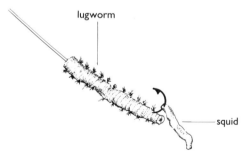

lugworm

squid

FIGURE 53   A mixed bait of lugworm and squid often proves deadly for sea bream.

combination bait. First I threaded a big black lugworm over the hook and up the line. Next I tipped the hook point with a slim section of squid (see Fig. 53). The second this cocktail touched bottom a fish took it hard, rattling the light rod tip in unmistakable bream style. Hooking this fish was easy and I got two more in quick succession before anyone asked what bait I was using. Once I had

explained the double bait, it was, as they say, 'a fish a chuck'. With an agreed bag limit of four fish, though, it was soon a switch to catch and release for everyone. Since that day I have used the cocktail bait many times, always with great success.

On light tackle, black bream are one of the hardest fighting fish on the British list. This 4 lb 12 oz (2 kg) specimen is close to maximum size for the species.

RED BREAM

More of a deep-water species than the black bream, immature red bream will come inshore but once a certain size is reached these beautiful fish vanish again to live over deep reefs and wrecks. Red bream provide first-class sport and also make extremely good table fish. Essentially they are a West Country species, rarely found east of the mid-Channel buoy. Generally, the further west you go the more common these fish become. When I was a boy it was possible to fish at night for red bream from the lighthouse quay at Mevagissey. In those days the local fish cannery dumped tons of fish offal from the quay, and this constant supply of food brought many kinds of fish to the quay head. The red bream, known as 'chad', appeared just before dark. On a good night it was possible to catch them by the dozen. The technique was to float-fish with a fish strip bait set about 6 ft (1.8 m) below the float. Once the bait was in position the line between the rod tip and the float was tightened up so that bites could be felt easily. In those days we took this magical style of fishing for granted. Now, it is long gone, except from the memories of anglers like me, who found it some of the best fishing of our young lives.

Today, red bream are caught only from deep water. Few anglers specialize in this species, but those who do enjoy good sport. Like the black bream, red bream are best caught on paternoster tackle. But unlike the normally finicky black bream, the red is a bold-biting fish with little apparent fear of even the crudest of terminal tackle. A simple but effective set of end tackle can be made by cutting a set of four or six mackerel feathers. These should be baited with fish or squid strip. Once red bream locate a bait they normally snap it up, often hooking themselves. Like the black bream, the red bream has a tough mouth and very few fish shake free of the hook.

Large red bream are now rare, but several much rarer species of bream occasionally occur in British waters. The most common of these are gilthead bream and Ray's bream. Most gilthead bream are caught by shore anglers. Ray's bream is more of an offshore fish (and there is some doubt as to its actual species).

13

Shark

For the angler interested in big, hard-fighting fish, shark are the obvious target. Four varieties are found in British waters: the blue shark, the porbeagle shark, the mako shark and the thresher shark.

BLUE SHARK

In the water, the blue shark looks like a fast, aggressive fish. Its appearance is deceptive, however, for once hooked most blue shark put up a poor fight, although a very big specimen may make several hard, fast and long runs before being brought to the boat. Sadly, most blue shark caught off Britain and Ireland weigh less than 65 lb (29.4 kg). Blues of over 110 lb (50 kg) are extremely rare. For many years the traditional Cornish blue shark grounds have fished poorly. In recent seasons, however, this downward trend has been reversed and the blue shark catches have shown a marked increase, not only in numbers of fish recorded but also in individual weights, several shark of over 130 lb (59 kg) having been taken. Obviously some change in the Atlantic current has brought blue shark into the lower Channel. Let us hope that this trend continues. In years gone by individual specimens of over 200 lb (91 kg) have been reported from Cornish waters, and further out in the Atlantic blue shark of more than 440 lb (200 kg) are far from unknown. Perhaps a few of these huge blues will eventually appear off Britain's coast. If they do, anglers will find out the difference in fighting power between an average and a large blue shark.

Although not a true shoal fish, blue shark tend to swim in loose packs. Catches of 30 or more blue shark in one day by a single boat were once common. Normally, where you locate one blue shark you will find others. In West Country waters the blue shark grounds are located 10–15 miles (16–24 km) offshore. The majority of West Country and Irish blue shark are caught by holiday makers, novice anglers who book a seat on a crowded shark-fishing

BLUE SHARK

This streamlined species gets its name from its distinctive dark-blue back and light-blue sides. These beautiful colours fade to a drab grey once the fish has been killed. It is an open-sea species, seldom venturing close to the shore. Blue shark weighing over 200 lb (91 kg) have been caught in British waters off Cornwall, and there is evidence to show that these fish can exceed 300 lb (136 kg). However, the average weight of rod-caught blue shark is less than 60 lb (27.2 kg) and many fish of around 40 lb (18.1 kg) are caught each season. The minimum qualifying weight for membership of the Shark Club of Great Britain is 75 lb (34 kg), and any fish topping 100 lb (45 kg) can be regarded as a good catch.

Few experienced shark fishermen regard blue shark as a sporting proposition. The knowledgeable angler usually goes blue sharking with a set of fairly light tackle in an attempt to get some reasonable sport from any fish that is hooked. For the novice shark angler, however, blue shark are any ideal species to start with. Two seasons of fishing for them are enough time to develop the skills necessary for pursuing the more hard-hitting porbeagle, mako and thresher shark.

expedition where everyone fights a shark in a strict rotation of rod sharing. Few knowledgeable shark anglers fish in this way. If they do, they tend to book a boat for a maximum of four rods and take their fish on far lighter tackle than that used by the daytrippers.

In British waters, blue shark are essentially a fish of the south and south-west. Occasionally, the odd specimen is recorded off Dorset but this would appear to be the up-Channel limit. Off Ireland, blues are found all round the south and west coast, and in these waters they tend to come in closer than they do around Britain, often approaching to within 2–3 miles (3–5 km) of the shore.

PORBEAGLE

Without question the most popular British shark, the porbeagle is big, hard-hitting and aggressive. It has a much wider distribution than the blue shark, being found from the Shetland Islands to the north coast of Cornwall. Essentially a pack shark, porbeagle can reach weights of more than 440 lb (200 kg). The average rod-caught specimen weighs 165–220 lb (75–100 kg). The first big catches of British porbeagle were taken off the Isle of Wight. The hotspot was on either side of St Catherine's Deeps, an area subject to an extremely hard tidal flow. Here the big porbeagle collected to massacre the shoals of tide-swept mackerel. In its heyday this area could produce individual boat catches of up to 12 big shark in one day. Many of the local fish were huge, and every shark angler who fished the area had his own personal 'lost monster' story.

PORBEAGLE

We still know very little about these fish, although it is certain that 'beagles' weighing at least 500 lb (227 kg) live and hunt in Britain's seas. It is also possible that much larger fish are yet to be detected in these waters. Unlike blue shark, which swim and feed well away from land, porbeagle tend to cruise close to the shore in search of food. A number of big porbeagle have been taken from the shore – all, remarkably, by float fishing with a beach-casting rod and 18–20 lb (8.2–9.1 kg) breaking strain line.

As a sporting species, the porbeagle has much to offer. A beautiful fish, its thick, muscular body and long fins give it a powerful appearance. The porbeagle's grey-brown back and large, muscular tail make it easy to distinguish from the blue shark. Any angler lucky enough to make contact with a specimen weighing over 100 lb (45 kg) will soon realize just how much strength and endurance a big 'beagle' can muster. There is no comparison between this fish and the far less exciting blue shark, for a porbeagle in good condition can provide even an expert angler with some truly thrilling sport.

Some of the really large St Catherine's sharks seemed to lead a charmed life. I recall a day out on a private boat, when I was there both to fish and find fish – a working holiday which gave me the opportunity to use my own tackle. We had judged our time of arrival to coincide with the start of the flood tide. The plan was to start some 2½ miles (4 km) off St Catherine's Point and drift eastward as far as Dunnose Head. We could then drift back westward on the ebb tide. This would give us the opportunity to fish twice through the most productive area. As usual, we used partly inflated balloons to support our double mackerel baits. It was a typically grey Channel day; a lot of cloud cover, but little wind. We had high hopes of early success, but the shark thought otherwise. The eastward drift proved negative. This was a disappointment, since we had drifted over the most productive area.

The rubby-dubby bag was constantly replenished with an obnoxiously over-ripe mixture of mashed mackerel, bran and liberal doses of a highly potent

Porbeagle shark can be caught from Shetland to the Scilly Isles. Always a hard-fighting species, most porbeagle are caught on large bait – a typical bait is double mackerel.

pilchard oil. The resulting oil slick could be seen disappearing into the distance; a wide smell lane made doubly attractive by the constant movement of thousands of mackerel and big garfish. These fish practically fought each other for the fish bits drifting out of the mesh 'dubby' bag. Their frantic movement alone should have been enough to attract shark but it didn't – at least not until just after slack water. As the boat was starting westward, a huge shark surfaced right beside my balloon float and I knew exactly what was going to happen next. Porbeagle shark seem to enjoy playing with floating objects. This one saw the balloon as a toy, twice nosing it clear out of the water. On the third occasion it made contact, and the balloon burst, scraped either by the shark's rough skin or a tooth.

Puzzled by the bang, the shark rolled completely over, giving us all a clear view of its length and breadth. To say it was a monster would be no exaggeration. Our conservative estimate of its weight was 550 lb (249 kg). A fraction of a second after it vanished, my big reel started to screech. I have never seen a shark in British waters take line so far and so fast. Within seconds it had over 200 yards (182 m) of 80 lb (36.2 kg) Dacron off the reel spool, and still it took line. At this stage I was confident that it had picked up the bait on its downward

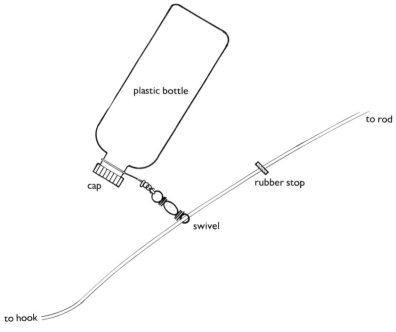

FIGURE 54 A cheap, efficient and easy-to-make shark float constructed from an empty plastic bottle, a short length of old line, a rubber stop and a swivel.

plunge and had hooked itself in the process. Suddenly the line went slack and the monster was gone. When I wound in, I found the Dacron frayed in a number of places. Obviously the porbeagle had not taken the bait, but had instead run it into the line. Typically, it had then automatically rolled and wound itself up in the line. Moments later its rough skin had chafed through the Dacron and it was free. Later that day I caught a 209 lb (95 kg) fish which looked tiny beside the lost monster.

In recent seasons, some huge porbeagles have been caught in Shetland waters. Again, the largest of the hooked fish have managed to come off before they could be gaffed. Unlike the blue shark, porbeagle tend to live and feed close to the coast. I have caught shark off Ventnor close enough to the beach to hear radios. In Ireland, the late Jack Shire, actually caught a number of large porbeagle while rock fishing – proof that they come right inshore to feed.

MAKO SHARK

The mako roves the world's oceans and when it appears in British waters provides all the thrills of true, big-game fishing. A hooked mako has been described as 'blue dynamite', a perfect description of this huge, high-leaping, beautiful shark. A close relative of the great white shark, the mako is a killer. In many parts of the world it is a known man-eater, afraid of nothing. In the vastness of the Atlantic, large mako prey on the equally formidable broadbill swordfish. In 1988 I saw a mako caught which weighed over 660 lb (299 kg). It had already killed and partly eaten a broadbill swordfish larger than itself.

The few mako that stray into British waters feed mostly on reef and wreck species, such as ling, pollack, cod and conger. The current British record mako had a 45 lb (20 kg) conger in its stomach. Eyewitness accounts of mako lost off Cornwall indicate that fish of up to 850 lb (385 kg) occasionally occur in those waters. No mako has yet been caught east of Devon's Start Point. Mako have been caught off Looe and Mevagissey, but undoubtedly the most productive Cornish port has been Falmouth – further proof that mako do not venture far up the English Channel. No mako have ever been reported from the Irish shark grounds, which is strange, given that the south and west coastline of Ireland faces the Atlantic. I suspect that mako are present but that Irish skippers and customers do not know where and when to find them. Mako like up-thrust rocks and shallow reefs. These fish are seldom found over the open-ocean ground favoured by the blue shark packs. I am sure that in time Irish waters will yield some mighty mako catches. Then, the shark-boat skippers will forsake their normal grounds to fish round rocky islands where the tide-rips boil their way through deep, dark water. Falmouth skippers caught most of the mako very near to the Manacles Reef, and off south and west Ireland many similar places wait to be fished.

MAKO SHARK

The aristocrat of the shark family, the mako is a handsome, streamlined, nomadic fish, highly sought after by game anglers the world over. Mako shark have been caught for many years in the English Channel and misidentified as porbeagle. In 1956 the teeth from a 'record porbeagle' were sent to the International Game Fish Association in the USA, where they were identified as mako teeth. An Atlantic fish that occasionally ventures into the mouth of the English Channel, the mako may well reach weights of over 700 lb (317 kg).

I have caught many huge mako in various parts of the world and through these encounters have come to regard it as the most sporting of the sharks. Unlike the blue and porbeagle sharks, the mako is a jumping fish, shooting out of the water like a guided missile, to fall back with a splash that can be heard for miles. Most of the mako I have caught in foreign waters have fallen to livebait. I have had the occasional specimen on dead fish, but these ocean rangers prefer their food live, and it doesn't seem to matter what the bait is. I have had mako on live mackerel, horse mackerel and, in particular, big and very lively red bream. When a hungry mako sweeps in to take a livebait there is no preliminary inspection. It hits the frantically swimming prey hard and fast, causing the reel to scream as it powers off with the bait. The shark must be given time to pouch the bait. At the first bite

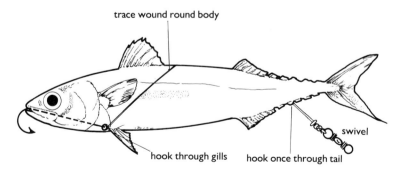

FIGURE 55 One way of hooking a shark bait is to pass the hook through the tail section, wrap the trace round the body of the bait and pass the hook through the gills so that the point and bend project from the bait's mouth.

indication, the rod point should be lowered to the angle of the running line. At the same time the check of the reel should be switched off, so that the shark can take line easily.

All shark bites follow a similar pattern. The fish picks up the bait and then makes a first run before slowing down to swallow it. The strike must be timed to coincide with the start of the second run. Too much delay and the fish will be gut-hooked. Very occasionally, a mako swallows the bait on the run. Once it is apparent that the shark is not going to slow down, the reel should be put into gear and the angler should brace himself for the powerful shock. Under these conditions, striking is out of the question. The impact is more than enough to set the hook.

THRESHER SHARK

Like the mako, the thresher is a jumping shark. Those I have caught or seen caught have repeatedly bounced out of the water like a rubber ball. When these tactics fail, the shark dives deep in an attempt to shed the hook. The name 'thresher' is derived from the shark's habit of threshing the surface water with its tail, an activity designed to panic the mackerel shoals on which it feeds. Once, I saw several thresher employing this tactic. It was a spectacular sight, with hundreds of frightened mackerel in the air at one time. Presumably the sharks find easy pickings among the disorganized shoal fish.

Few thresher shark are caught deliberately, the main reason being that few

---

THRESHER SHARK

A very distinctive fish, the thresher has a rakish appearance, owing to the upper lobe of the tail being almost as long as its body. Thresher are more common in European waters than is generally supposed, but no one can say for certain how prolific the species is, for the thresher is almost exclusively a bottom feeder and only occasionally appears on the surface.

For the rod-and-line angler, the thresher is a game and gallant opponent. Those that are hooked usually fall to conventional off-the-bottom shark-fishing techniques. However, true bottom fishing is the only practical way to catch thresher regularly. Specimens to just under 300 lb (136 kg) have been caught on rod and line, but it seems likely that, in European waters, threshers can reach at least 800 lb (363 kg).

Thresher shark reach
weights of over 300 lb
(136 kg). This little fish
took a bait intended for
tope. Hooked thresher
often jump clean out of
the water when hooked.

anglers understand where, when and how to catch these lovely creatures. Found all round the British Isles, the thresher is a shallow-water species. Probably the most productive grounds in Britain are round the Isle of Wight. During late July and August huge females come inshore to give birth. The best places to try are Sandown Bay and off Freshwater on the south and south-western side of the island. Huge fish are often sighted and occasionally hooked there, and I have seen thresher shark which I estimated to weigh over 440 lb (200 kg) in both areas. I was present when local angler John Roberts lost a monster in the closing stages of the battle. The fish had been on for about an hour before it was discovered that the boat's shark gaff had been stolen. A gaff was hastily improvised from a mop handle and a 12–0 shark hook. It was hoped that this would hold the fish long enough for a wire tail rope to be slid over the fish. John's shark was obviously exhausted and came in easily to the makeshift gaff. But the moment the hook sank into its flesh, it went crazy, ripped the hook off its handle and dived under the boat. Instantly, the taut line touched the keel and parted. The lost fish was huge and obviously a record breaker. We could only hope that it would manage to shed the hook and trace and live to fight another day.

I am certain that more thresher would be taken if anglers fished in the shallower, sandy-bottomed bays. The use of livebaits would probably also produce more takes. The first thresher I ever caught came by accident on a porbeagle trip. I had two customers out with me and had set one's baited tackle at 30 ft (9 m) and the other's at 60 ft (18 m). Bait fish had been scarce and I had used the four fresh mackerel we had caught on the way out. Now my customers suggested I put on my own tackle. I had plenty of deep-frozen mackerel and I chose a large fish as bait. It was still stiff and coated with ice as I slipped it over the side. I had set the orange balloon at 45 ft (14 m) to fish the bait between the other anglers' balloons. As my balloon drew level with the other two it shot out of sight at high speed. The other two baits were immediately wound in out of harm's way. Seconds later, the fish came back directly under the boat's transom. I knew that I would never have a better chance to set the hook.

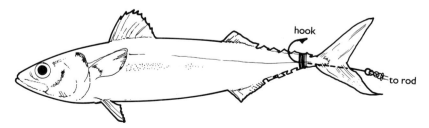

FIGURE 56 Another simpler way of hooking a shark bait is to pass the hook through the tail section of the bait, then lash the wrist of the tail to the hook with wire, wool or elastic.

When I struck, the fish was directly below the rod tip. It didn't stay there long. Feeling the hook, it came straight out of the water. At the time we had *Angling Times* photographer Bill Goddard on board. Five times the fish jumped and five times Bill tried to catch the jump on film. Later, we found he had missed the fish completely. After its fifth jump, the thresher went deep and soon succumbed to heavy rod pressure. When we came to gaff it, it brought its great tail into play. Each time someone leaned out with the gaff, the tail came whistling through the air to thump down hard on the gunnel; an unusual but none the less effective tactic to keep us from using the gaff. Finally, however, it was over and the fish was inboard.

Since catching that first thresher, I have studied their habits and distribution and believe that there are far more of these sporting sharks around than most anglers realize.

Once exclusively a West Country sport, shark fishing has spread all over Britain. The headquarters of the Shark Club of Great Britain is still based in Looe, in Cornwall, but its members come from all over. Sharking is justly popular, for anglers from all walks of life can afford a place on a charter boat. In this way the novice shark angler gets a chance to contact and fight a battle he will never forget. Aptly, shark have been described as 'the poor man's big-game fish'.

TACKLE

Rods

It is customary for shark charter boats to carry a selection of rods, reels and traces for hire, an arrangement which is ideal for the novice. By catching a few fish on hired tackle, the inexperienced angler can decide on just what outfit to purchase. Hire rods are often heavy for the average run of sharks. Fortunately, most anglers realize this and when buying an outfit of their own, normally pick a lighter rod. Most tackle firms and specialist rodmakers produce fibreglass and carbon/glass rods which conform to the standards laid down for shark fishing by the IGFA (International Game Fish Association). The 50 lb (22.6 kg) and 80 lb (36.2 kg) class rods are ideal. The former is perfect for all aspects of blue shark, while the heavier rod is best suited to porbeagle, mako and thresher shark. The quoted poundage (or kilogram equivalent) indicates the breaking strain of line which can be safely used with the rod.

When choosing a shark rod, pay particular attention to the rings and the reel seat. Most manufacturers produce well-fitted rods, but there are still a few that skimp on quality. I prefer rods fitted with a full set of AFTCO roller rings. American-made, these are the best rollers in the world. They have been copied, but to an inferior standard. Reel fittings should also be of the highest quality. A combination of corrosive salt water and a succession of big fish soon show up any defects in the metalwork fitted to a rod. Basically, you get what you pay for. Cheap rods and big fish are a bad combination. If in doubt about what is on offer, or to save money, make up your own rod by purchasing the blank and the fittings you require. Shark rods are not difficult to put together and a home-built rod, apart from being made to your own requirements, will save you a lot of money.

Reels

Choosing a reel for shark fishing is never easy. A wide variety of such reels is available, some fitted with the old-fashioned star drag system, others with state-of-the-art lever drags. The Penn Company of America make the best and most robust star drag multiplying reels. For blue shark a Penn Senator 6–0 is a good choice. For the other three species a Senator 9–0 is better in that it has greater line capacity. When it comes to ultra-modern and highly efficient lever drags reels, then Japanese companies lead the field. The ideal Shimano reels for sharking are the TLD 25 or the more expensive 50 class Beastmaster. Both models have won a top name for themselves worldwide. For the angler who finds such reels too expensive when new, it is wise to shop around for a good secondhand reel. The angling newspapers and magazines have used-tackle columns that often feature shark reels at half the price of a new reel.

Line

The breaking strain of the line you purchase must match the rod you intend to use. For example, with a 50 lb (22.6 kg) class rod a line of similar breaking strain should be used. The best lines conform to IGFA ratings. This means that they are pre-tested to break at below the rated figure. For example, 80 lb (36.2 kg) breaking strain line breaks at 72 lb (32.7 kg). Cheap, unrated lines are not pre-tested and may well break below the printed breaking strain. A record shark caught on unrated line may well be disqualified when the line is tested by the British Record Fish Committee. The two types of line commonly used for shark fishing are nylon and Dacron. Both have their advantages and disadvantages. Nylon, for example, is extremely elastic, stretching under pressure. Dacron, a weaker line of man-made fibre, is buoyant and does not suffer from stretch. The main disadvantage of Dacron is that it will break instantly if it comes into contact with anything solid while under pressure; if, for example, it brushes a second shark while you are playing a hooked fish. Plain nylon is much harder, but it absorbs water and sinks. This can be a major problem, for as the line between rod tip and trace sinks it may well cross the baited trace. If this occurs, a taking shark can easily pick up both bait and reel line. For this reason it is better to use nylon without any form of float. In this way the weight of the bait and the flow of the tide keeps the line taught at all times. Nylon can be knotted with a standard tucked blood knot. Dacron is very different. Knotted Dacron can easily cut itself under pressure. To avoid this, the line should be hitched with a hangman's jam.

Traces

Shark have extremely sharp teeth which can cut or saw through line and, in some instances, wire. To avoid losing fish it is essential to construct the trace from the best available material. My own traces, made from galvanized yacht-rigging wire, comprise two sections, joined by a single large swivel. Any good yacht chandler will provide both the wire and the crimps that hold the swivels and hooks in place, and will have the machinery to put the crimps in place (see Fig. 57). When making up a trace, make sure that no wire ends are left protruding from the crimps, for in use these ends will fray out, and in this state they are extremely dangerous. Never use nylon-coated wire. The coating will catch on a shark's teeth, and once this happens the teeth will lock into position and rapidly saw through the wire inside.

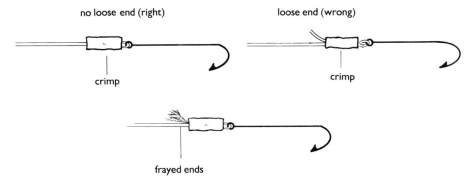

FIGURE 57 A good trace can be made from 15 feet (4.6 m) of 'rigging wire' available from a chandler. To strengthen the trace, use crimps at both the hook and swivel end of the wire. These should be fitted professionally by the chandler. When having a crimp fitted, make sure that it covers the loose end of the wire, otherwise the wire will fray and may inflict a nasty gash.

Hooks

The world's finest shark hook is the chromium-plated Mustad Seamaster. For use in British waters, these hooks in size 10–0 or 12–0 are sufficient. Although extremely strong, with a well-sharpened point, Seamaster hooks must be carefully honed with a file and carborundum stone. First, the file is used to shape the hook point, and the stone is then used to finish off the curved edge of the hook point.

Swivels

Trace swivels have to withstand abnormal pressures. For this reason, only the finest quality swivels should be used. The two most reliable patterns are the Berkley barrel swivel and the much more expensive Sampo ball swivel. Cheap barrel swivels have a nasty habit of straightening out under pressure.

14

Tope

The tope is a fast-moving, hard-hitting little shark that offers the chance of catching a big fish without incurring the expense of a shark trip. Most large tope are females, the majority of male tope weighing 20–30 lb (9.1–13.6 kg). In recent seasons, however, some exceptionally large males have been caught off St Catherine's lighthouse, on the Isle of Wight, where fish of up to 50 lb (22.6 kg) have been recorded. Male tope are normally found in huge packs, while females are solitary. You may well catch two or three large females from one mark, but each fish will be there for food rather than for companionship.

Twenty years ago Britain's tope population suffered a massive decline. In those days anglers brought all their own tope ashore for photographs and weighing, a practice which soon destroyed many once fine tope marks. Fortunately, anglers and club officials came to realize that tope were rapidly becoming an endangered species. Conservation practices were adopted and now tope stocks are finally re-established. Killing tope is in any case pointless, for while they are a pleasure to catch, they make very poor eating. During the past few summers huge bands of tope have established themselves in the overfalls area of St Catherine's Deeps. In this part of the English Channel the tides are invariably savage. Slack water is of short duration, and the fish seem to feed at any stage of the tide. Shoals of mackerel recognize the area as a well-stocked larder and it is these fish that bring the predators into the area. Once famous for the quality of its porbeagle shark, the area is now making a comeback with its tope. Catches of over 80 rod-caught tope per boat have been recorded in a single day's fishing. Most of the fish weigh about 20 lb (9.1 kg), but sprinkled among them are a few much larger fish.

The last time I fished St Catherine's Deeps, I was aboard the Lymington boat *Private Venture*. Its skipper, Chris Savage, knows the area intimately. He was confident of catching fish but he warned us that the tides would be savage and that wire line was therefore the order of the day. Tope are generally thought of as a bottom-feeding fish, but there are times when they will feed just under the

Hard fighters, tope can be guaranteed to provide first class sport. This fine 48-pounder (21.8 kg) was released seconds after the picture was taken. Most anglers nowadays automatically release any tope they catch.

surface. When I was shark fishing professionally there were many days when tope fed voraciously in the rubby-dubby slick. So persistent were they that more than once I had to give up sharking for the day. Now, I was out fishing the same area with tope rather than shark as the target species. The tackle was a simple one-hook running leger with a wire trace and a well-sharpened size 8–0 flat-forged O'Shaughnessy hook. The bait was the head end of a fresh mackerel cut on the angle to retain the guts. A bait cut in this way lays its own scent trail, which we knew would quickly bring the tope to investigate our hook baits.

Within minutes the first fish were on the scene, and on the hooks. Three out of six of us were into fish before the first tope was tailed out of the water. The other three rods were bent down hard in their battle curves. From this time on, wave after wave of medium-sized tope took our baits. Baits were frequently picked off 'on the drop', a sure sign that the tope pack was rising up from the sea bed. To try and get through these smaller tope I doubled the size of my lead and sent a big bait down fast. The trick worked and I made contact with a fish of a different calibre. To begin with, it had things its own way, running out a great deal of wire as it hurtled away down-tide. A good-sized tope in full flight can take some stopping. The secret is to let it take line, but only under pressure. A fish played in this way may take 50 yards (46 m) or more of line. But then it will tire and turn against the pressure from the line and rod. Once it starts to swing back it is essential to crank the reel handle as fast as possible. Contact must be maintained at all time. These tactics fluster the fish into circling directly under the rod tip. At this stage the fish can be easily worked to the surface. Increasing the rod pressure will make the fish spiral upwards. This was achieved easily and as it came up we could see that it was a male, and a big one at that. As Chris tailed it into the boat we could see that it weighed well over 40 lb (18.1 kg). It was a thick-set, broad-nosed powerhouse of a fish. With the hook neatly in the corner of its trap-like mouth, it was the work of seconds to remove it. After a couple of quick photographs the tope was slid gently back into the water, probably no worse for its experience.

At that time this fish was the largest male tope I had ever seen. Minutes later I saw a bigger one. The angler fishing beside me struck into a good fish which fought with the style and speed typical of the tope. Finally, it was in sight and as it surfaced we could see it was a monster of a male. Again, it was mouth-hooked. We did not weigh it, but it was easily a 50-pounder (22.6 kg). As usual, though, the fish was photographed and carefully returned. Chris and I agreed that in all probability neither of us would ever see such a pair of male tope again. Oddly enough, we did not catch another tope that day. Instead, a snake's nest of good-sized conger came on the feed.

TOPE

A small member of the shark family popular with British anglers, the tope has a typically shark-like appearance, with two dorsal fins and prominent gill slits. Its big tail has a deeply notched upper lobe, and the fish has a grey or greyish-brown back and white underparts.

The average weight of a rod-caught tope is about 30 lb (13.6 kg), but fish of 45 lb (20.4 kg) are by no means exceptional. The record rod-caught tope weighed over 70 lb (31.8 kg), a fair indication that the species can reach a much greater weight in British waters.

Contrary to popular belief, tope are not confined to Britain's south and south-western coastline. They have a wide distribution and are very common on the Essex coast, and some large catches are taken each year from this area. Further north, they are rarely caught, until one gets as far as Scotland. In Luce Bay and around the Scottish islands, these fish are often very common. They can be caught almost anywhere around Britain, provided that anglers are prepared to use the right tackle and bait.

Tope are a summer species, the best catches being made from June until the end of September. The first tope catches are often made about mid May, and June and July are the most productive months. Large tope have been caught in December and January, however, on baits intended for cod. Tope may be classed as game fish, for although most anglers encounter the odd fish that gives up without a struggle, the majority put up a determined battle.

Most tope are caught on cut or filleted fish and traditionally mackerel is the best bait. Certainly tope find the oily flesh of mackerel highly attractive, but it is a mistake to regard mackerel as the only successful tope bait. Tope are hunters who live a hit-and-run existence, taking food where and when they can find it. In the natural state they have no time to be choosy – a fish is a meal irrespective of species. Pouting, for example, are an excellent tope bait, but small whiting are just as good. Herring are always worth a try, but they must be fresh. Far too many anglers rely on baits which have spent months in a freezer. Fish do not freeze well and the oily-fleshed mackerel and herring quickly start to rot from the inside out. Under any conditions a correctly presented live fish will attract and catch tope faster than any dead fish bait, whether whole or cut.

LIVEBAITING

Livebaits are best fished on a long, flowing trace of 6–8 ft (1.8–2.4 m). This length allows the livebait to swim up from the sea bed. To get the best out of a livebait it should be hooked through the wrist of the tail (see Fig. 58). It is important to pass the hook through the bait's flesh, for if it touches the backbone it will cripple the fish. Tope hunt by sight and smell, and by picking up vibration patterns. A bait hooked through the tail root will be forced to turn back into the tide flow. To maintain its position it will then have to swim hard and this sends out the sort of vibrations that hungry tope soon pick up.

At various times when tope have been active I have fished livebaits while other anglers have stuck to dead fish. Every time, the livebait has produced far more than the dead bait. The bites on a livebait are of the tearaway kind. The fish obviously sweep in fast, grab the swimming bait and carry it off at high speed. With a cut bait there are normally some preliminary warning knocks on the rod tip. The smash-and-grab take on livebait, however, can take you by surprise. For

FIGURE 58 Hook a livebait through the tail wrist. Pouting made good livebait for tope. Squid and cuttlefish are also a favourite although most tope fall to mackerel or herring baits.

this reason the rod should be held at all times, with the reel out of gear but on ratchet. When a fish picks up the bait it must be allowed to run off with it, for tope are extremely cautious. I normally switch off the ratchet as soon as the fish starts to run, controlling the line by light thumb pressure. Normally the fish will take 20–30 yards (18.2–27.4 m) of line and then slow down, or even stop, to swallow the bait. As soon as it begins to run for the second time I engage the spool, wait for the weight of the fish to drag the rod tip down and simply lift into the running fish. If you time the strike to coincide with the start of the second run, the tope is likely to be mouth-hooked. Any delay will result in a throat or gut-hooked fish.

SHORE FISHING

There was a time when shore fishing for tope was a viable proposition in many areas. The Welsh coast, Parkshore on the Solent, and many other locations produced superb sport. Unfortunately, inshore pollution and overkilling by anglers destroyed many of the most productive areas. Tope can still be caught from one or two West Country headlands and steep-to-shingle banks such as Dorset's Chesil beach. In these areas tope are more plentiful than most anglers realize. The best months are June, July and August, when the mackerel shoals maraud inshore to harry the shoaling sand eel and the diminutive brit. The tope follow the mackerel and a big bait presented in the right place can produce the fish of a lifetime. A good-sized tope hooked on a standard beach-casting outfit can put up a spectacular battle. I have had hooked fish tear off 100 yards (91 m) of line in seconds. On one occasion I even had a fish totally 'spool' me, taking all the line off my reel before breaking the reel knot. For shore fishing, large dead sand eels or the tail half of a mackerel make the best baits. These should be fished on a leger rig which incorporates an anti-tangle tube (see Fig. 59). This tubing is obtainable from any good tackle stockist. Inshore tope are best caught on multiplying reels. Even the largest fixed-spool reels are not strong enough to last long when tope are the quarry.

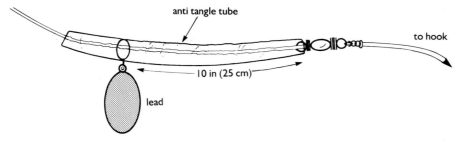

FIGURE 59   An anti-tangle tube. A trace of 2–3 feet (0.6–0.9 m) is best used with a forged hook.

15

Whiting and Haddock

WHITING

Popular with both beach and boat anglers, the whiting is a game little fish which makes a welcome and tasty addition to any catch. A true member of the cod family, it is often called Channel whiting or simply Channel. Most anglers regard it as a winter species, and in most of Britain this is true. Down in Cornwall, however, whiting are a fish of high summer. In the days when I did a lot of blue shark fishing off south Cornwall, I always took a light rod along to catch whiting. Cornish whiting are good-sized fish, and to get the best sport I used a single French boom to present the bait paternoster-style (see Fig. 60) 3 ft (0.9 m) or so off the sea bed. The bait was inevitably fresh mackerel strip. Active hunters, offshore whiting seem to prefer a fish bait to any other offering. Whiting bite with a distinctive sharp, tugging action, and left alone they normally swallow the bait, hooking themselves. On days when they are finicky it pays to wind in slowly at the fist sign of a bite. This will normally encourage the fish to swallow the bait.

In Cornish waters the whiting average 2½–3 lb (1.1–1.4 kg). Further up the Channel, however, where whiting are definitely a winter species, fish of 5 lb (2.3 kg) or more can often be caught. My favourite area for whiting is south of the Needles lighthouse, where the big 'Channels' live and feed with the cod packs. The unusual thing about whiting in this area is that they mainly feed during the slack-water period. At this time the cod seem to take a rest, leaving the whiting to glut themselves. Vast shoals of sprat appear off the island during the winter, and these provide the whiting with rich pickings. As a hook bait, sprat tends to be too soft, the sharp teeth of the whiting turning it into instant fish paste. For this reason, fish-strip baits are normally used. Whiting can be taken on running leger tackle, but for the best results a one- or two-hook nylon or metal boomed paternoster should be used. Like most predatory fish, whiting hunt by a combination of sight, smell, and vibration directions. To draw fish

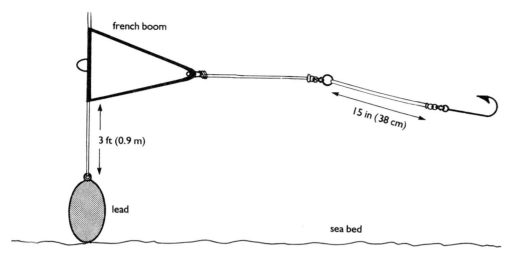

french boom

15 in (38 cm)

3 ft (0.9 m)

lead

sea bed

FIGURE 60 Small fish form the main diet of this predatory species, although they feed from the bottom as well. A French boom keeps the bait clear of the sea bed.

into the area of your baits, try raising and lowering the rod tip several times. This causes the lead to bump repeatedly on the bottom, a technique which often produces bites instantly. I have used this trick for many years and have proved over and over again that it helps hunting fish to home in on the suspended baits.

Beach fishing

Whiting are by no means an exclusive offshore species. From the shingle beaches of Dorset, Sussex, and Kent up to the flatter beaches of Suffolk and Norfolk, they offer first-class sport to the beach angler. Beach fishing for whiting is essentially a nocturnal occupation. In deeper offshore waters whiting feed at any time of the day, but over shallow inshore feeding areas they seldom appear until well after dark. A popular winter beach is often packed to capacity, so it pays to arrive early and stake your claim. Once night falls and the Tilley lamps are glowing, the beach takes on something of a festive air.

The secret of successful sport with inshore whiting is the bait. Deep-water fish are less selective than their inshore cousins. Fish is what they expect, whereas inshore whiting are more likely to be interested in worm, specifically black lugworm. The angler with the best bait usually walks off the beach with the best catch. For beach casting, where long casts are essential, the terminal tackle is normally reduced to the bare essentials. The bait is still fished on a paternoster rig, but the cumbersome French boom is discarded in favour of a nylon rig (see Fig. 61) which presents the bait well but offers the minimum air resistance during casting. For this sort of fishing a standard 12 ft (3.6 m) beach rod capable of casting 2–6 oz (60–170 g) is perfect. The reel can be a small multiplier or a large fixed-spool, depending on personal preference. Line breaking strain should be 15–18 lb (6.8–8.2 kg). A 30 ft (9 m) length of 25–30 lb (11.3–13.6 kg) shock leader should be used at all times. This is tied directly to the reel line and acts as a shock absorber during casting. This is an important part of any beach angler's standard rig. A 'crack off' is dangerous, but using a shock leader will cut the risk of this happening to a minimum.

Sometimes the whiting appear in vast numbers, setting every rod tip on the beach jigging as the fish snatch frantically at every bait. I remember fishing a well-known Suffolk shingle beach on one such night. This was a long-planned expedition, for which vast amounts of black lugworm had been ordered and collected. For good measure I had a cool box full of fresh herring. Rods, reel, lines, traces and shock leaders had been checked. Everything was as ready as it would ever be. I arrived to find the beach well populated, for the venue had been fishing well for several weeks, and both local and visiting anglers had heard the news. By the time twilight arrived I had everything set up. Rod rests were firmly implanted. Rods were propped ready, bait to hand, the lamp lit, and my giant green 'brolly' pegged down as a windshield. The chill factor of a winter North Sea wind is savage and the umbrella made all the difference between total discomfort and the prospect of a pleasant night.

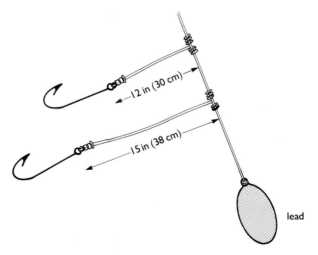

FIGURE 61   A two-hook nylon paternoster for beach fishing. Use light tackle. If whiting grew as large as cod they would provide incredible sport: as it is, a 2 lb (0.9 kg) whiting is a reasonable fish.

Channel whiting rarely reach a weight of more than 5 lb (2.3 kg). This fish is about 2 lb (0.9 kg). Always popular, whiting are hard biters that are justifiably popular with boat and beach anglers alike.

WHITING

If whiting grew to the size of cod they would be marvellous to catch on rod and line, for their streamlined body and rather pointed head give them a much greater turn of speed. Unfortunately, the average whiting caught in British waters weighs only 1½–2 lb (0.7–0.9 kg), and a fish of double this weight may be regarded as a large specimen.

Whiting have a very wide distribution, and can only be caught from one end of the British Isles to the other. They are a winter species, although boat anglers who fish deep marks well offshore often catch large bags of good-sized whiting during the summer and autumn. One look at the tooth-filled mouth of the whiting reveals that it is a predator. Small live fish form the basic diet, but whiting often resort to bottom feeding as well. Because of this, they can be caught on almost any natural bait. The majority of the large whiting taken fall to sprat baits. Long strips of squid, cut to resemble a sand eel, also produce good results, as do fish-strip baits.

Since whiting generally feed just off the sea bed, a light two- or three-hook paternoster rig is probably the best terminal tackle to use for boat fishing.

Just before darkness set in I baited up both rods with bunched lugworm. The baits had not been out for more than ten minutes when both rod tips began to nod. A wave of fish had obviously swept inshore and the whole beach had become a hive of activity. Winding in as fast as I could, I beached two fat whiting, dropped the rod and picked up the second pole. Again I had two fish. Judging by the activity all around me, everyone was experiencing similar sport. Abandoning the two-rod set-up, I rebaited just one set of hooks. Seconds after the bait hit the water I was into yet another brace of whiting.

One hour and some 30 whiting later, the fish were still on the move. At this stage I stopped counting. Even with only one rod in use I was running out of what I had thought was an adequate supply of worms. Soon even the last worm fragments were gone and I was forced to change to herring strip. The fish did not want it. They were obviously still preoccupied with worm, for the fish strip produced only the odd bite. I had intended making a night of it, but by 10 o'clock my sport had finished. I had a bumper catch of fish but would have preferred it if they had been spread over a longer period of time. I spent the remainder of the night asleep in the car.

HADDOCK

Of similar size to the whiting, haddock are striking little fish. As a species they are confined to the extremities of the British Isles. Mainly a northern fish, they also occur in isolated groups off the south of Cornwall. Southern haddock have a much larger average size than their northern counterparts. If I had to pinpoint one mark capable of producing a record haddock it would be the 'field', a muddy sand hole situated off Dodman Head, south of Mevagissey, in Cornwall. This mark does not produce many haddock in a season but the ones that do get caught usually weigh between 7 and 10 lb (3.2 and 4.5 kg). In northern waters a 6 lb (2.7 kg) specimen would be huge, but in Cornwall it would not raise an eyebrow.

HADDOCK

Although haddock were once widely distributed around Britain, commercial over-fishing has now made them rare for, like whiting, they are a good table fish. To catch haddock in any quantity on rod and line it is necessary to fish off the west coast of Scotland. The largest haddock come from Cornish marks, where specimens of over 10 lb (4.5 kg) are often encountered.

Haddock are closely related to cod and there is a strong similarity in appearance. The haddock can be distinguished from the cod, however, by its slightly forked tail, black lateral line and dark spot either side of its body. These fish are exclusively bottom feeders and although they will eat small fish if they can catch them, their diet is mainly marine worms, crustacea, starfish and various molluscs. Whiting tackle is best for haddock fishing, and most of the fish I have taken fell to fish or squid-strip baits.

Like the whiting, haddock are best fished for just above the sea bed with a one or two-hook paternoster rig. One of the best places I have fished for this species was a bank off Portrush, on the Antrim coast of Northern Ireland. The favoured bait here was a cocktail of worm and fish strip. The area was solid with haddock, most of them weighing about 2 lb (0.9 kg). The occasional fish of 4½–5 lb (2–2.3 kg) also turned up to add a little extra excitement. Catches of over 100 fish were common. The mark was deep but not subject to a heavy tide flow, which made it possible to use light tackle. However, a number of fish tore off the hooks on the way up to the boat. Notoriously soft-mouthed, haddock are easily lost in this way. To overcome the problem we used a Japanese gadget called a rubber swivel as a buffer between the terminal tackle and the reel line. This device consists of 6 in (15 cm) of orange industrial rubber with a swivel at each end. Under pressure of a hooked fish the rubber stretches sufficiently to stop the fish tearing free. Modern chemically sharpened hooks are also useful in this respect. The fine wire and ultra-sharp point produce only a small hole, making it difficult for a hooked fish to wriggle off.

Haddock are rarely encountered by the beach angler, although at one time they could be caught from shore marks round the Isle of Arran. The bait in this area was scallop. Normally confined to specific areas, haddock occasionally undergo a population explosion. When this occurs they appear in areas well beyond their normal range. The last time this happened haddock invaded the Thames estuary and as far along the Channel as the Isle of Wight.

When it comes to tackle for haddock and whiting most anglers use their existing beach and boat gear. To get the best out of boat fishing a 12 lb (5.4 kg) class rod is ideal. Such a rod gives perfect bite indication and makes it possible to fish light enough to enjoy the fighting spirit of both species.

16

Wrasse

Since my childhood wrasse have fascinated me. Once regarded as little more than bait-robbing vermin, these lovely rock fish have finally come of age. Once, each fish would be dumped on the rocks to flap out its life. Now, wrasse are fished for with respect, and returned alive to the sea. Wrasse fishing has become a specialized art. Anglers travel long distances in search of specimen or possibly record-breaking wrasse. From the sporting point of view only one species of British wrasse is of interest. This is the ballan wrasse, which can exceed 10 or even 12 lb (4.5 or 5.4 kg). Most rod caught specimens weigh between 2¼ and 5 lb (1 and 2.3 kg). A 6-pounder (2.7 kg) is a good catch and anything over 7 lb (3.2 kg) can be classed as the fish of a lifetime.

WRASSE

Several species of wrasse are found around the coast of the British Isles, but it is the ballan wrasse that is of most interest to the angler. This fish has a deep, solid-looking body, a long, spiky dorsal fin and neat, strong white teeth. The coloration is extremely variable, the commonest colours being brown or greenish-brown. The belly and head of the adult fish are in many cases netted with red or orange-red scales, each of which has a light centre spot.

To get the best out of wrasse fishing, it pays to fish as light as possible. No special tackle is required, bass-strength gear being ideal for general wrasse sport.

Many years ago I caught a 9¾ lb (4.4 kg) fish from a gully on the east side of Chapel Point, South Cornwall. Big as the fish was, it did not qualify as a record breaker, for at that time the record stood at 12¾ lb (5.8 kg). Years after my catch the existing record fish was found in a glass case. Measurements taken from the mounted fish proved that it originally weighed between 6 and 7 lb

(2.7 and 3.2 kg). Once it was revealed as a fake the original record was removed from the lists and left open at 8 lb (3.6 kg). It now stands at 8 lb 6 oz (3.8 kg), a record which is wide open to attack.

To catch big wrasse it is essential to know the fish and understand their habits. Wrasse are essentially an inshore rock fish. Their preferred haunts are deep-water gullies with a heavy growth of kelp weed. Ballan wrasse use this weed both as shelter and as a rich feeding ground. It is only necessary to look at the heavy armour-like scales of a big wrasse to know that it is very well equipped for life in heavy seas and rocky conditions. Its mouth is fleshy, with strong, rubbery lips and a solid display of white peg-like teeth. Big wrasse will occasionally take a sand eel or other small fish, but they are not by nature predatory. Their main intake of food consists of worms, prawns, crabs and shellfish. From the specialist angler's point of view, the hard-backed green shore crab is the only bait to use. Worm, prawn and deshelled limpet or mussel can be relied on to catch more wrasse than crab bait, but they will be of a much smaller average size. It is really up to the angler to decide whether he wants to catch a lot of medium-sized wrasse or the odd whopper.

Knowing what bait to use is only part of the battle. Small ballan wrasse are everywhere where there is sufficient rock to provide them with shelter. I have caught them in waters ranging from the west coast of Scotland down to the Scilly Isles. The west coast of Ireland is thick with them. But big wrasse are very different. Never common, they may exist in only one or two places in many miles of what seems like the ideal sort of coast for wrasse. In my own experience the place to look for an outsized wrasse is a deep gully that never fully dries out. The gully should either be flanked on both sides by high rock or have a bottom comprised of deep, rocky canyons grown over with thick kelp weed; almost the sort of place to try inshore conger fishing. I like a gully which only partly dries out, for each outgoing tide strands and kills endless prawn and crabs. When the tide starts to flood such edible flotsam drifts back into deep water like a natural groundbait. Resident wrasse take full advantage of this natural food supply. A hook baited with crab and dropped into the gully will usually be snatched up by the first wrasse that sees it. There are a number of places round Britain's southern coastlines where a record-breaking specimen is possible. The best known is the Pulpit Rock area of Portland Bill, in Dorset. Local spearfishers are said to have speared ballan wrasse to 15 lb (6.8 kg) round the base of these rocks. Certainly the area has produced some hefty wrasse. Crab, as usual, has been the most productive bait. Trevose Head in North Cornwall has also given up some big fish. South Cornwall, from Mevagissey to the Lizard Point, is worth investigating, as are the Scilly Isles. The south-western coast of Ireland is a wrasse angler's paradise, the only problem being to wade through the medium weights before finding those extra-large fish.

Wrasse are often the mainstay of the rock fisherman's sport. Hard hitting, hard fighting, these wrasse can reach a weight in excess of 8 lb (3.6 kg).

PATERNOSTERING

I remember a trip to Dingle in Co. Kerry. I found a mark on Slea Head which could only be reached with difficulty. This hole was less than 200 yards (183 m) from a great, flat rock slab capable of producing wrasse by the thousand. To my knowledge, it had never been fished. To get down to it I had to slither down a rock slope to a narrow, very uncomfortable ledge which fell sheer away into dark, very obviously deep water. The place screamed conger but I knew from past experience that inshore conger and very big wrasse show a liking for the same holes. Maybe the reason the wrasse grow big is that the conger kill off many small ones. The survivors fatten up on the extra food and soon reach a weight that makes them too big for smallish eels to tackle.

My favourite terminal tackle for wrasse fishing is a simple one-hook paternoster. This is formed by sliding a size 1–0 or 2–0 hook onto the reel line. The line is then doubled and a series of simple overhand knots are tied in to form a stiff double line (see Fig. 62). This arrangement keeps the dangling bait from twisting back round the reel line. The weight is attached to the bottom of the reel line by means of a rubber band (see Fig. 63). The weight can be an old spark plug or a link of chain. If it gets snagged the band will snap and the rest of the terminal tackle will be saved. I picked up this tip from Alderney angler Roddy Hayes. Most garages are happy to give you a regular supply of used spark plugs. In this instance the garage in Dingle had come up trumps. I had enough disposable weights and enough hard crab for a marathon session. I was fishing with heavy gear, for a big wrasse hooked in a snag-filled area can make mincemeat out of light or medium-weight tackle. My rod was a powerful bass pole fitted with an extremely free-running multiplying reel loaded with 30 lb (13.6 kg) line. This may sound ultra-strong for a fish which may at best weigh 7 or 8 lb (3.2 or 3.6 kg). Believe me, it is not. A big wrasse has to be stopped in its tracks. Give it the smallest amount of line and it will go instantly to ground. I know several Channel Islands wrasse anglers who fish 40 lb (18.1 kg) reel line as standard. Even using this they have been 'snapped off' by unstoppable wrasse.

Having found the safest part of the ledge, I baited up with a crab about 2 in (5 cm) across. I hooked the crab through the belly flap so the point of the hook came out of its back (see Fig. 64). This gives a solid hook hold and presents the crab in a natural position. As the bait hit the surface and vanished from sight I knew instinctively that this hole could be a Klondyke. Minutes passed without a touch. Twice I lifted the rod tip to move the bait to a new area, all to no avail.

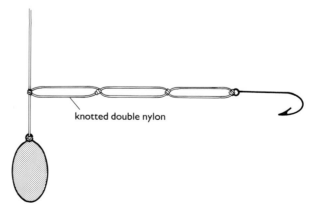

knotted double nylon

FIGURE 62   A 'heavy nylon' paternoster for wrasse. This variation on the French boom works well and keeps the bait away from hungry crabs. Fish with 15–20 lb (7–9 kg) line, for a ballan wrasse can be a hard-fighting fish.

Twenty minutes later I retrieved to cast further along the rock wall at my feet. As the bait hit bottom and the line tightened I felt the double knock of a biting fish. As always, I waited for the follow-up pull. Nothing happened. After a five-minute pause I wound in to find my bait gone. It takes a good wrasse to chew off a big crab in two bites and I cursed my luck in having missed it. Still, I had plenty of time and ample bait.

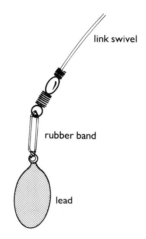

FIGURE 63   Use a rubber band to join a lead to a link swivel. This can save your terminal tackle when over rock.

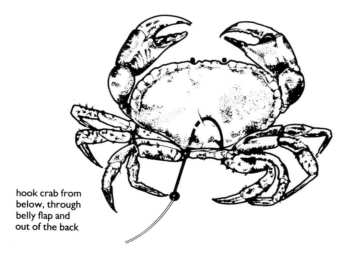

FIGURE 64   Baiting with crab. Limpets, prawns and worms are also successful. Big wrasse will also take small fish and sand eels.

Having put on a slightly smaller crab, I made my second cast of the day. The bait dropped to within a foot (0.3 m) of where my first cast had landed. This time I was ready. The second the rod tip nodded I struck. Instantly the hooked fish reacted by plunging for the security of some undersea cavern. This was 'hold on and haul' time. One of us had to win and I intended it to be me. Everything held. The fish surged round virtually under the rod tip, but did not reach cover. I have found that if you defeat a wrasse on its first explosive dive it usually gives in within minutes. This fish was typical. It tried twice more to get its head down and when this failed it simply gave up. On the scales it weighed exactly 7 lb (3.2 kg); my best Irish wrasse to date. With luck this new-found gully would soon give me a bigger one.

During the next hour I missed two bites and landed two more fish, a brace of fat 5-pounders (2.3 kg) that could have been one and the same fish except for a colour difference. Each fish had been returned straight after weighing and I was having doubts about whether I could hook a better fish than my 7-pounder (3.2 kg). As a final gesture I hooked on the largest crab in my bait bag. If there was a monster down in that dark water surely a crab of this size would draw it out. What happened next is something I shall never forget. The bait had been in position for about five minutes before the rod tip rapped twice and then slammed down hard. The bite said wrasse; the fight did not. At first the fish tried a crash dive. When this failed it moved diagonally away like a ship under sail. Finally, it turned and swept out into deep water, snapping the line. I still dream about that fish. It could have been a huge bass. But I doubt it. The bite and initial plunge was all wrasse. I know it was the wrasse of my lifetime, but as for its weight, I would not like to guess. Very big and very strong; a wrasse that might have put me in the record book for the next hundred years or so. A miss is as good as a mile, but I cannot help wondering. I fished the same spot three more times. I got one of my 5-pounders (2.3 kg) again, recognizing it by a hook mark in its lip. Try as I might, however, I never touched the monster again.

FLOAT FISHING

Whether you take wrasse seriously or not, it does not matter. They are a joy to catch and provide first-class sport for expert and amateur alike. One of the nicest, although not necessarily the most effective, ways to fish for them is with float tackle. To get the best out of this style of angling a streamlined pike-style float should be used (see Fig. 65). This type of float is constructed round a central tube through which the line passes. It may seem strange to use a pike float for sea fishing but most sea floats are too big and bulky. A small section of rubber band hitched onto the reel line above the float acts as an easily adjustable stop. The float should be set so that the bait hangs 10–12 in (25–30 cm) above the bottom. Remember, however, that most rock gullies have ledges and deep drop-offs. This is where the float becomes inefficient. It may present the bait perfectly at one moment. The next the bait may well be several feet above the feeding fish (see Fig. 66). None the less to watch the float jiggle and bob to a wrasse bite is fascinating.

I have had many great days wrasse fishing. These fish normally live in wild, lonely areas where the scenery is as important as the fishing. My favourite spot is Alderney, in the Channel Islands. It is an angler's paradise, and although only a small island, it has dozens of wrasse marks, many capable of producing very big

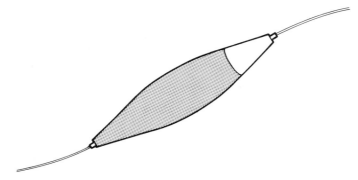

FIGURE 65   A pike-style float. Wrasse are a rock-haunting species so it pays to fish 12 inches or so (0.3 m) off the sea bed.

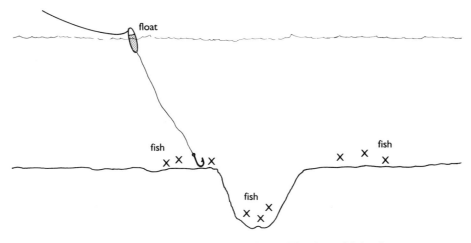

FIGURE 66   When the float passes over a hole, the bait will be above fish level.

fish. I was out on one occasion with local anglers Roddy Hayes and Rob Labalistair, who had decided to show me a favourite mark. To get to the fishing area was a rather interesting exercise in itself. First, we drove down a very badly constructed track which ultimately petered out, with no apparent way to the sea. Shouldering our gear, we scrambled over an area of loose stones and there in front was the entrance to a wartime gun emplacement. Without hesitation the lads entered this black hole. Feeling our way through several corridors, we came at last to the gun position. The gun was gone but the gun slit was still in place. Through this narrow and awkward exit we went and I found myself on a broad, flat ledge at the base of a tall cliff. This, then, was our fishing position, attainable only by way of the gun emplacement.

Rob and Roddy were like pair of excited children. This was obviously a favourite place and one which they assured me could easily produce very big wrasse. With ample bait we intended to fish the tide up and halfway down again. Our tackle was heavy: beach casting rods and 30 lb (13.6 kg) line. The terminal tackle was basic: a single-hook nylon paternoster with a spark plug held by a rubber band as a weight. Tackle losses at this spot were normally high, so we had dozens of used spark plugs with us. We didn't know it then, but it was going to be Rob's day. As we made our first casts there was the usual banter. A pint of beer on the first fish. Hardly had Roddy offered the wager than Rob hit that first fish, an attractive red and turquoise 4½-pounder (2 kg) that was quickly netted, unhooked and returned alive. Next, I got a smaller fish. Then Rob had a superb 6-pounder (2.7 kg). I can remember photographing this fish and thinking to myself that whatever happened the day was made already. Rob obviously did not agree. Ten minutes after his 6-pounder (2.7 kg) he hit a huge fish which weighed in at 7 lb 12 oz (3.5 kg), just 12 oz (0.3 kg) short of the British record. Unfortunately, this was last of the big fish for the day. We went on to catch plenty of medium-weight specimens, fish that kept our rod tips rattling until the falling tide caused them to stop feeding. Several weeks later I heard that Rob had been back to the gun emplacement and had caught a wrasse of 8 lb 3 oz (3.7 kg). Could his next fish break the record?

Primarily a shore fish, ballan wrasse can be taken by boat anglers operating within 200–300 yards (183–274 m) of the coastline. This is beyond normal casting range and well inside the areas fished by the charter boats. A sort of unfished no man's land which can and does produce excellent wrasse catches for the dinghy angler. It is this sort of unfished strip that might well produce a few monster ballan wrasse. Remember, however, that wrasse like to live and feed in depths of up to 8–10 fathoms (14.7–18.2 m). Beyond this the only type of wrasse you will encounter is the exceedingly beautiful but rather small cuckoo wrasse. Pick an area where the bottom is a jumble of rocks and thick weed and success with the ballan wrasse is almost guaranteed.

Index

Numbers in *italic* refer to illustrations